HOW TO
WRITE RIGHT 2

Forms and More

Eleanor Segan

Illustrations by
Barbara Slate

ENTRY PUBLISHING, INC.
NEW YORK, NY

Eleanor Segan has taught language arts and reading for more than 20 years in both New Jersey public schools and New York City public schools. She has been a teacher trainer in both systems, preparing teachers to teach reading and writing skills. Ms. Segan authored Language Arts for the Open Classroom for the state of New Jersey.

Acknowledgements

My thanks to all those who helped me, most especially to my family for their suggestions, contributions and patience;

to Lynne Glasner, my publisher, for her additions and continuous support;

to Barbara Slate, whose illustrations in this book added life and humor;

to Gloria Sigman, for her gracious cooperation;

to Lynn Haney of Citibank, for her many helpful suggestions;

and finally, to Steve Jobs, whose dedication to the development of the Macintosh computer made it possible for me to write these books.

Eleanor Segan

Dedication

To my mother, Pessie Klein, in loving memory

E.S.

Writing Skills Series
How to Write Right 1: From Lists to Letters
How to Write Right 2: Forms and More

Cover design by Barbara Slate
Book design and typesetting by Robert Schaffel

ISBN 0-941342-14-X (Writing Skills Series)
ISBN 0-941342-16-6 How to Write Right 2: Forms and More

Entry Publishing, Inc.
27 West 96 Street
New York, NY 10025

Printed in the United States of America
0 9 8 7 6 5 4 3

Table of Contents

Introduction

Do you like to fill out forms? No? Well, you are like a lot of other people. Most of us don't like forms.

Some people say that the questions are too hard. Some say that the words are too hard. And some people say that the forms are too long.

Did you know that many forms have been changed? They were too hard for everyone! Now they are easier.

If so many of us don't like filling out forms, why do we have to do it?

There are good reasons.

Forms tell a lot about us. When you go for a job, the company wants to know about you. The boss must know where you live. He or she must know what work you have done and what you do best. You fill out a form.

You go to open a bank account. The bank must know where you live and where you work. They want to know many other things about you. You fill out a form. Your boss and the bank will keep your forms. They will look at them many times.

You will have to fill out many forms in your life. Some are short and easy. Some will take more time.

This book will help you. And so will Formal Ike. Ike gets a little bossy sometimes. But he only wants to help.

> **DON'T BE AFRAID TO ASK QUESTIONS. NOBODY KNOWS EVERYTHING!**

About Filling Out Forms

- Have a pencil, pen and eraser with you.

- Print everything. Use handwriting only when you sign your name.

- First fill out the form lightly in pencil. Erase any mistakes. Then go over the whole thing neatly with a pen. Or, get two forms. Practice on one. Fill in the good copy in ink and hand it in.

- Fill in everything that you know.

- Ask for help with the parts that you don't understand.

1   Information Sheet

Forms ask for a lot of information about you. It is hard to remember lots of numbers, dates, and addresses. But you can be ready to fill out most forms.

Look at the Information Sheet on pages 5 and 6. It has blank spaces now. As you read this book, you will fill in most of the blank spaces. Later on, you will fill in more spaces by yourself. You may change or add some things as time goes by. Always add the newest information to keep your Information Sheet up to date.

Take this Information Sheet with you. Use it when you have to fill out a form. Copy the information from your own Information Sheet onto the right places on the form.

INFORMATION SHEET
ALL ABOUT ME!

NAME: FORMAL IKE

ADDRESS: 1 PRIM PATH
PROPER CITY, ME
04666

BIRTH DATE: APRIL 1, 1948

HEIGHT: 3'11"
WEIGHT: 80 LBS.

EYE COLOR: BABY BLUE

HAIR COLOR: BALD

Information Sheet

Name: First _____   Middle _____   Last_____

Address   _____   _____
             (number/street)   *(apt. no.)*

            _____   _____
             (city/state)   *(zip code)*

Soc. Sec. No. _____/_____/_____ Home Tel: area code (____)_____

Birth date_____, 19_____   Birth Date _____/_____/_____

Driver's License No. _____

Height _____ Weight _____ Eye Color _____ Hair Color _____

Family Doctor _____ Tel. No.: area code (____)_____

Name of Bank _____

Address _____ Zip Code _____

Type of Account

      Savings____ Account No. _____ Checking____ Account No. _____

Education—Start with the last school that you attended.

School Name _____ City _____ State ____

      From (date) _____/_____/_____   to (date) _____/_____/_____

School Name _____ City _____ State ____

      From (date) _____/_____/_____   to (date) _____/_____/_____

Jobs

I work for _____

Address _____ Zip Code _____

Tel No.: area code (____)_____ Supervisor's Name _____

My job is _____

Other Jobs I Have Had

1. Company Name _____

    From (date) _____/_____/_____   to (date) _____/_____/_____

    Address _____ Zip Code _____

Tel No.: area code (____)_____ Supervisor's Name _____

My job was _____

2. Company Name _____

    From (date) _____/_____/_____   to (date) _____/_____/_____

    Address _____ Zip Code _____

Tel No.: area code (____)_____ Supervisor's Name _____

My job was _____

Personal References

1. Name _____ Tel No.: area code (____)_____

    Address _____ Zip Code _____

2. Name _____ Tel No.: area code (____)_____

    Address _____ Zip Code _____

3. Name _____ Tel No.: area code (____)_____

    Address _____ Zip Code _____

Other Information That I Need

_____

_____

_____

2   Writing about You

Forms ask you to write many things about yourself. Sometimes, this information is called **personal data**. The personal data on a form tells the reader who you are.

Your Name

The first space on a form asks for your name. Forms are not all the same. Some ask you to print your first name first. Some ask for your last name first.

Look at the name and **signature** forms below.

Form A

Name		
(First)	(Middle)	(Last)
Nick	Evan	Turner

Signature
Nick Evan Turner

Form B

Name Turner   Nick   Evan
      Last   First   Middle

Signed *Nick Evan Turner*

Form C

Name Nick   E.   Turner
      (First) (Middle Initial) (Last)

Signature *Nick Evan Turner*

Formal Ike

7

In Form A, Nick had to print his name on a line **under** the words <u>First</u>, <u>Middle</u>, and <u>Last</u>.

In Forms B and C, Nick had to print his name **above** the words <u>First</u>, <u>Middle</u>, and <u>Last</u>.

NOTE: Look at Nick's signature on the forms. It is always the same.

Practice

Fill in these name forms. Use your own name.

Name

(First)   (Middle)   (Last)

_____

Signature

_____

Name _____

(Last)   (First)   (Middle Initial)

Signature _____

Name _____

(First)   (Middle Initial)   (Last)

Signature _____

Look at your name forms again. Did you fill them in the right way? If not, go back and write it right.

Now turn to the Information Sheet on page 5. Fill in your name.

Some forms have boxes. Look at the name form below. Ann Marie Alter has filled it in.

Name (Last, First, Middle Initial)

| A | L | T | E | R | | A | N | N | | M | | | | | |

Ann left one empty box after her last name and one empty box after her first name. She did not fill in the spaces after her middle **initial**.

Your name may be very long. Fill in all the boxes. Then stop. Don't write where there are no boxes.

Henrietta Pressamonte filled in a name form. It looked like this.

Name (Last, First, Middle Initial)

| P | r | e | s | s | a | m | o | n | t | e | | H | e | n | r | ietta J |

Henrietta did not write it right. Henrietta's whole name will not fit in the boxes. She must leave out some letters of her first name and her middle initial.

Practice

Fill in this name form for Henrietta Pressamonte.

Name (Last, First, Middle Initial)

| | | | | | | | | | | | | | | | | | | |

Print your name neatly on the form below.

Name (Last, First, Middle Initial)

| | | | | | | | | | | | | | | | | | | |

Look at your name forms again. Did you fill them in the right way? If not, go back and write it right.

Your Address and Telephone Number

The next part of a form asks for your address.

Look at Ed Pepper's address on the form below.

222 File St.	Power City	MA 01202
Address—Number and Street	City or Town	State Zip Code

Ed printed the abbreviation for Massachusetts. The abbreviations for all the states are on the last page of this book. Always write your zip code after the state name. If you don't know the zip code for your address, call the post office.

Practice

Print your address on these forms.

Home Address

Number and Street	City or Town	State	Zip Code

Home Address

Now write your telephone number on the line below. Every phone number starts with an area code. Write that first. If you don't know your area code, call your telephone company or look on your phone bill.

Telephone Number area code (_____) _____

Look at your address and telephone number forms. Did you fill them in the right way? If not, go back and write it right.

Now turn to page 5 and print your address and telephone number on your Information Sheet.

The Date

Most forms have a space for the date. The date is the month, day, and year now. It is the day that you are filling out the form.

Spaces for the date may be different on different forms. Look at the space for the date on the forms below.

> **A.** Date _____
>
> **B.** Date _____ , 19_____

In A, you must write the month, day, and year on one long line. In B, the month and the day are printed on the long line. The year number is after the <u>19</u>.

September 3, 1988 looks like this.

> Date _September 3, 1988_____
>
> Date _September 3_____ , 19**88**__

Print today's date in the spaces below.

> Date _____
>
> Date _____ , 19_____

Some forms ask for the date a different way. You may have to write the date in numbers only.

Every month has a number. January is number 1 because it is the first month of the year. December is number 12 because it is the last month of the year.

The number of the month goes in the first space. Write the day of the month in the middle space. Write the last two numbers of the year in the last space. September 3, 1988 looks like this.

> _9_ / _3_ / _88_

July 18, 1988 looks like this.

> _7_ / _18_ / _88_

NUMBERS OF THE MONTHS	
January	1
February	2
March	3
April	4
May	5
June	6
July	7
August	8
September	9
October	10
November	11
December	12

Practice

Write these dates in numbers. Use the spaces below.

April 15, 1987   _____/_____/_____

September 2, 1988   _____/_____/_____

February 23, 1989   _____/_____/_____

Look at the dates again. Did you put the right numbers in the right spaces? If not, go back and write it right.

Other Information about You

Many forms ask other questions about you. They may ask how old you are. They may ask what you look like. They may ask for your birth date. Your birth date is the month, day, and year that you were born.

Some forms ask you to write out the name of the month and then the other number. Some forms ask for the month, day and year only in numbers.

Vera Ramos was born on February 11, 1968. Look at one part of a form that Vera filled out.

Another form had a different kind of space. So Vera filled it in with numbers only.

Date of Birth
February 11 _____, 19 68

_____2___,__11__,__68__
Month   Day   Year

The birth date on Vera's forms

Practice

Write your birth date in the spaces below. In the first space, write out the name of the month. In the other spaces, write the month, day, and year in numbers only.

Date of Birth_____, 19_____

Date of Birth_____/_____/_____

_____/_____/_____
Month   Day   Year

Be careful! You were not born this year.

Look at your date of birth forms. Did you fill in the right date? If not, go back and write it right.

Now print your birth date on your Information Sheet on page 5. Write it two ways.
    1. Write out the month and then the other numbers.
    2. Write it in numbers only.

Other questions on forms may be about what you look like. Many times the forms use abbreviations for these parts.

Look at a form that Vera filled out.

Date of Birth 2 / 11 / 68			
5'5"	125 lbs.	Brown	Black
Ht.	Wt.	Eye Color	Hair Color

NOTE: You can find a list of Abbreviations on the last page of this book.

Vera is 5 feet 5 inches tall. She wrote 5' 5" because ' stands for feet and " stands for inches. She filled in her weight and used the abbreviation for pounds. Then she wrote her eye color and hair color.

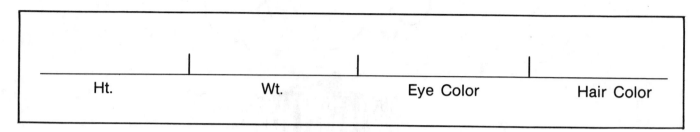

Practice

Fill in this form about what you look like.

| Ht. | Wt. | Eye Color | Hair Color |

Check Yourself

Look at your form again. Did you fill it in the right way? Let's see.

Answer these questions. Mark Yes or No.

	YES	NO
1. Did you fill in all the parts?	☐	☐
2. Is your printing easy to read?	☐	☐
3. Did you use the abbreviations for your height and weight?	☐	☐

Now turn to your Information Sheet on page 5. Fill in your weight, height, eye color, and hair color.

3   Social Security Card Application

Are you looking for a job? You will need to get a Social Security card first.

Here's how to get one.

Look in the telephone book under Social Security Administration. You will find the address and telephone number there. Go to the nearest Social Security office. Take **identification** papers with you. These papers prove who you are and how old you are. You may take school records, your birth certificate, or other identification. Take your Information Sheet with you, too.

Ask for a Social Security application form. Fill it out. Give it back and show your identification papers. That is all that you must do.

About five weeks later, you will get your Social Security card in the mail. Sign it and put it in a safe place with other important papers.

The number on the card is the important thing. No one else has that number. **Try to remember it without looking at the card**.

You will need to use your Social Security number many times in your life. You will have to write this number on many forms.

Take care of your card. If you lose your card, you will have to fill out a form again.

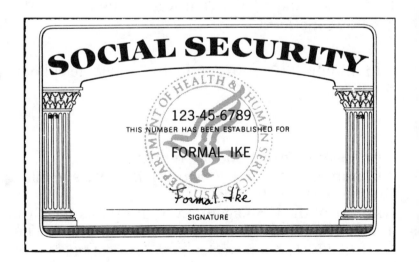

The Social Security card application form has 14 parts or items. Each part has numbers and letters in boxes.

Ann Alter filled out a form before she got her first job. Look at Ann's form on page 17.

In number 1, Ann filled out only the first line. She has never used any other names. So she drew lines like this ——— in the other parts of number 1. These parts have nothing to do with Ann.

Ann filled in her address in number 2 and checked the right boxes in number 3 and number 4.

Number 5 says Voluntary. This means that Ann does not have to answer this question. She left it blank.

For number 6, Ann wrote her birth date in numbers. For number 7, she wrote her age in years. For number 8, she wrote out the city and state of her birth. She did not use abbreviations because the form says Do Not Abbreviate.

Number 9 asks about Ann's parents. Ann filled in their names.

In number 10, Ann checked No because she had never applied for a card before. So she did not need to fill out the rest of number 10. She went on to number 11. It says Today's date. That was the date that Ann filled out the form.

In number 12, Ann wrote her home telephone number.

Ann signed her name for number 13.

In number 14, Ann checked Self because she filled out the form for herself.

Ann read the form again. Everything was filled in. It was neat. She gave it to a clerk at the Social Security office. A few weeks later, Ann got her Social Security card in the mail.

DEPARTMENT OF HEALTH AND HUMAN SERVICES
SOCIAL SECURITY ADMINISTRATION

Form Approved
OMB No. 0960-006

FORM SS-5 – APPLICATION FOR A SOCIAL SECURITY NUMBER CARD (Original, Replacement or Correction)

Unless the requested information is provided, we may not be able to issue a Social Security Number (20 CFR 422-103(b)).

INSTRUCTIONS TO APPLICANT ▶ Before completing this form, please read the instructions on the opposite page. Type or print, using pen with dark blue or black ink. Do not use pencil. SEE PAGE 1 FOR REQUIRED EVIDENCE.

NAA
NAB
1
ONA

NAME TO BE SHOWN ON CARD
First	Middle	Last
Ann	Marie	Alter

FULL NAME AT BIRTH (IF OTHER THAN ABOVE)
First	Middle	Last

OTHER NAME(S) USED

STT 2
MAILING ADDRESS (Street/Apt. No., P.O. Box, Rural Route No.)
88 Key Road   Apartment 4H

CTY
CITY (Do not abbreviate)	STE	STATE	ZIP	ZIP CODE
Power City		MA		01202

CSP 3 CITIZENSHIP (Check one only)
- ☒ a. U.S. citizen
- ☐ b. Legal alien allowed to work
- ☐ c. Legal alien not allowed to work
- ☐ d. Other (See instructions on Page 2)

SEX 4
- ☐ MALE
- ☒ FEMALE

ETB 5 RACE/ETHNIC DESCRIPTION (Check one only) (Voluntary)
- ☐ a. Asian, Asian-American or Pacific Islander (Includes persons of Chinese, Filipino, Japanese, Korean, Samoan, etc., ancestry or descent)
- ☐ b. Hispanic (Includes persons of Chicano, Cuban, Mexican or Mexican-American, Puerto Rican, South or Central American, or other Spanish ancestry or descent)
- ☐ c. Negro or Black (not Hispanic)
- ☐ d. Northern American Indian or Alaskan Native
- ☐ e. White (not Hispanic)

DOB 6 DATE OF BIRTH
MONTH	DAY	YEAR	AGE	PRESENT AGE
3	17	70	7	17

PLB 8 PLACE OF BIRTH ▶
CITY (Do not abbreviate)	STATE OR FOREIGN COUNTRY (Do not abbreviate)	FCI
Chicago	Illinois	☐

MNA 9 MOTHER'S NAME AT HER BIRTH
First	Middle	Last (Her maiden name)
Rona	Ida	Faro

FNA FATHER'S NAME
First	Middle	Last
John	—	Alter

PNO 10
a. Has a Social Security number card ever been requested for the person listed in item 1? ☐ YES(2) ☒ NO(1) ☐ Don't know(1)
b. Was a card received for the person listed in item 1? ☐ YES(3) ☐ NO(1) ☐ Don't know(1)

▶ IF YOU CHECKED YES TO A OR B, COMPLETE ITEMS C THROUGH E; OTHERWISE GO TO ITEM 11.

SSN
c. Enter the Social Security number assigned to the person listed in item 1. ☐☐☐ – ☐☐ – ☐☐☐☐

NLC
d. Enter the name shown on the most recent Social Security card issued for the person listed in item 1.

PDB
e. Date of birth correction (See Instruction 10 on page 2) ▶
MONTH	DAY	YEAR

DON 11 TODAY'S DATE ▶
MONTH	DAY	YEAR
4	21	1987

12 Telephone number where we can reach you during the day. Please include the area code.
HOME	OTHER
413-247-6161	

ASD WARNING: Deliberately furnishing (or causing to be furnished) false information on this application is a crime punishable by fine or imprisonment, or both.

IMPORTANT REMINDER: WE CANNOT PROCESS THIS APPLICATION WITHOUT THE REQUIRED EVIDENCE. SEE PAGE

13 YOUR SIGNATURE
Ann Marie Alter

14 YOUR RELATIONSHIP TO PERSON IN ITEM 1
☒ Self ☐ Other (Specify)

WITNESS (Needed only if signed by mark "X")   WITNESS (Needed only if signed by mark "X")

DO NOT WRITE BELOW THIS LINE (FOR SSA USE ONLY)

DTC (SSA RECEIPT DATE)	NPN	DOC

NTC	CAN	BIC	IDN	ITV	☐ MANDATORY IN PERSON INTERVIEW CONDUCTED

TYPE(S) OF EVIDENCE SUBMITTED

SIGNATURE AND TITLE OF EMPLOYEE(S) REVIEWING EVIDENCE AND/OR CONDUCTING INTERVIEW

DATE
DATE
DCL

FORM **SS-5** (1-85)   5/84 edition may be used until supply is exhausted

Practice

Fill out the Social Security application form on page19. If you do not know the answer to any item, print <u>unknown</u> in that space. Use your Information Sheet to help you.

You may take this form with you when you go to the Social Security office. You can also take your Information Sheet. Use these forms to help you fill out the form at the Social Security office. Do not hand in the form from this book.

DEPARTMENT OF HEALTH AND HUMAN SERVICES
SOCIAL SECURITY ADMINISTRATION

Form Approved
OMB No. 0960-0066

FORM SS-5 — APPLICATION FOR A SOCIAL SECURITY NUMBER CARD (Original, Replacement or Correction)

Unless the requested information is provided, we may not be able to issue a Social Security Number (20 CFR 422-103(b)).

INSTRUCTIONS TO APPLICANT ▶ Before completing this form, please read the instructions on the opposite page. Type or print, using pen with dark blue or black ink. Do not use pencil. SEE PAGE 1 FOR REQUIRED EVIDENCE.

		First	Middle	Last
NAA	NAME TO BE SHOWN ON CARD			
NAB 1	FULL NAME AT BIRTH (IF OTHER THAN ABOVE)	First	Middle	Last
ONA	OTHER NAME(S) USED			

STT 2 MAILING ADDRESS — (Street/Apt. No., P.O. Box, Rural Route No.)

CTY	CITY (Do not abbreviate)	STE	STATE	ZIP	ZIP CODE

CSP 3 CITIZENSHIP (Check one only)
- ☐ a. U.S. citizen
- ☐ b. Legal alien allowed to work
- ☐ c. Legal alien not allowed to work
- ☐ d. Other (See instructions on Page 2)

SEX 4
- ☐ MALE
- ☐ FEMALE

ETB 5 RACE/ETHNIC DESCRIPTION (Check one only) (Voluntary)
- ☐ a. Asian, Asian-American or Pacific Islander (Includes persons of Chinese, Filipino, Japanese, Korean, Samoan, etc., ancestry or descent)
- ☐ b. Hispanic (Includes persons of Chicano, Cuban, Mexican or Mexican-American, Puerto Rican, South or Central American, or other Spanish ancestry or descent)
- ☐ c. Negro or Black (not Hispanic)
- ☐ d. Northern American Indian or Alaskan Native
- ☐ e. White (not Hispanic)

DOB 6	DATE OF BIRTH ▶	MONTH	DAY	YEAR	AGE 7	PRESENT AGE	PLB 8	PLACE OF BIRTH ▶	CITY (Do not abbreviate)	STATE OR FOREIGN COUNTRY (Do not abbreviate)	FCI ☐

		First	Middle	Last (Her maiden name)
MNA 9	MOTHER'S NAME AT HER BIRTH			
FNA	FATHER'S NAME	First	Middle	Last

PNO 10
a. Has a Social Security number card ever been requested for the person listed in item 1? ☐ YES(2) ☐ NO(1) ☐ Don't know(1)

b. Was a card received for the person listed in item 1? ☐ YES(3) ☐ NO(1) ☐ Don't know(1)

▶ **IF YOU CHECKED YES TO A OR B, COMPLETE ITEMS C THROUGH E; OTHERWISE GO TO ITEM 11.**

SSN c. Enter the Social Security number assigned to the person listed in item 1. ☐☐☐ — ☐☐ — ☐☐☐☐

NLC d. Enter the name shown on the most recent Social Security card issued for the person listed in item 1.

PDB e. Date of birth correction (See Instruction 10 on page 2) ▶ MONTH DAY YEAR

DON 11	TODAY'S DATE ▶	MONTH	DAY	YEAR	12	Telephone number where we can reach you during the day. Please include the area code. ▶	HOME	OTHER

ASD WARNING: Deliberately furnishing (or causing to be furnished) false information on this application is a crime punishable by fine or imprisonment, or both.

IMPORTANT REMINDER: WE CANNOT PROCESS THIS APPLICATION WITHOUT THE REQUIRED EVIDENCE. SEE PAGE 1

13 YOUR SIGNATURE

14 YOUR RELATIONSHIP TO PERSON IN ITEM 1
☐ Self ☐ Other (Specify) _____

WITNESS (Needed only if signed by mark "X")

WITNESS (Needed only if signed by mark "X")

DO NOT WRITE BELOW THIS LINE (FOR SSA USE ONLY)

DTC (SSA RECEIPT DATE)	NPN	DOC

NTC	CAN		BIC	IDN	ITV	☐ MANDATORY IN PERSON INTERVIEW CONDUCTED

TYPE(S) OF EVIDENCE SUBMITTED

SIGNATURE AND TITLE OF EMPLOYEE(S) REVIEWING EVIDENCE AND/OR CONDUCTING INTERVIEW

DATE

DATE

DCL

Form SS-5 (8-85)
5/84 and 1/85 editions may be used until supply is exhausted

Check Yourself

Look at your Social Security card application form. Are you ready to hand it in?
Let's see.

Answer these questions. Mark Yes or No.   YES ✔ NO

1. Did you fill in all the parts that are about you?   □   □

2. Did you draw a line in any parts that have nothing to do with you?   □   □

3. Did you print <u>unknown</u> where you did not know the answer to any item? □   □

4. Did you sign the form on part <u>13</u>?   □   □

When you get your Social Security number, write it on your Information Sheet.

4 Job Application Forms

Important Words

Qualifications—things that you do well.
Position—job.
Legally eligible—allowed by law.
Rate of pay—how much money someone makes.
Specify—to tell exactly.
Previously—before this time.
Available—ready to start.
Salary—the amount of money paid for a job.
References—people who know you and can tell about you.
Employer—the person or company that you will be working for.
Occupation—the kind of work that you do.
Physical handicap—something wrong with your body.
Marital status—married, single, widowed, or divorced.
Referred by—the person who told you about this job or where you found out about it.

When you ask for a job, you may have to fill out a form. Someone from the company will read your form. This person will talk to you about the job.

A job application form and an employment application form are names for the same kind of forms. But all these forms do not look the same. Some are short, but most are long. They have many words that may be new to you. Some of those words are on the Important Words list for this chapter. Look also at the Glossary on page 60 and the list of Abbreviations on page 62.

About Job Applications

- Print neatly and clearly.
- You may see some parts that say For Office Use Only. Leave those parts blank. Fill in everything else.
- There may be some parts that have nothing to do with you. Put lines like this———in those spaces.
- Write Not Sure or Unknown if you don't know the answer to something.
- Ask for help if you don't understand a question.

Ed Pepper wants a job as a cook in the restaurant of a large company. He filled out an Application for Employment form. His Information Sheet helped him.

Look at Ed's form on pages 23 and 24. Let's see how he filled out some parts.

The first part is Personal. These are things about Ed. Some questions had nothing to do with Ed. He put lines in those spaces.

He did not write his age because he is not under 18 or older than 70. He put a line in that space.

He put Open after Rate of pay expected because he wanted to talk about that.

Ed can't start a new job right away. First he will have to tell his boss that he is leaving this job. Ed's boss will need some time to find another worker for Ed's job. So Ed wrote that he could start the new job in about three weeks.

Ed filled in all the schools that he went to. He wrote the name of the cooking school, too. This tells the company that he has learned how to cook and will be able to do the job.

In the Employment part, Ed wrote about his jobs. First he wrote the name and address of the job that he has now. He put a line in the space under To because he is still working at Abel Tool Company. Then he wrote about his past jobs. Ed only had one other job. So he crossed out the last spaces. He didn't want anyone to think that he forgot to fill in that part.

Ed looked at the next part. He didn't want another company to call his boss yet. First, he wanted to make sure that he had another job. Then Ed can tell Mr. Abel that he will leave his job in two weeks. Ed wrote about this on the form.

Ed gave three references. He did not write the names of relatives or anyone he has worked for.

Ed got to the last part. It said Please read and sign below. Ed didn't understand all of it. So he asked someone at the company for help. A worker helped him with that part of the form. Then Ed signed his name on the bottom.

APPLICATION FOR EMPLOYMENT

(PLEASE PRINT PLAINLY)

To Applicant: We deeply appreciate your interest in our organization and assure you that we are sincerely interested in your qualifications. A clear understanding of your background and work history will aid us in placing you in the position that best meets your qualifications *and* may assist us in possible future upgrading.

PERSONAL

Date **September 20, 1988**

Name **Pepper** **Edward** **—**
     Last   First   Middle

Social Security No. **230-21-8041**

Present address **222** **File St.** **Power City** **MA** **01202**
     No   Street   City   State   Zip

Telephone No. **(413)246·8015**

Are you legally eligible for employment in the U.S.A.? **Yes**

State age if under 18 or over 70. **—**

What method of transportation will you use to get to work? **bus**

Position(s) applied for **Cook**

Rate of pay expected $ **Open** per week

Were you previously employed by us? **No** If yes. when? **—**

If your application is considered favorably. on what date will you be available for work? **October 15** 19 **88**

Are there any other experiences, skills, or qualifications which you feel would especially fit you for work with our organization? **I do all my family's cooking at home. I went to cooking school for 1 year, at night.**

RECORD OF EDUCATION

School	Name and Address of School	Course of Study	Check Last Year Completed	Did You Graduate?	List Diploma or Degree
Elementary	Elm Street School Elm St. Appleton, WI 54914	✕	5 6 7 (8)	☑ Yes ☐ No	✕
High	Power City High School 200 High School Drive Power City, MA 01201	general	1 2 3 (4)	☑ Yes ☐ No	general
College	— — —		1 2 3 4	☐ Yes ☐ No	
Other (Specify)	Food Arts Cooking School 305 W. Walnut St. Chips, MA 02207	general cooking; grill	(1) 2 3 4	☑ Yes ☐ No	certificate

(Turn to Next Page)

List below all present and past employment, beginning with your most recent

I

Name and Address of Company and Type of Business	From		To		Weekly Starting Salary	Weekly Last Salary	Reason for Leaving	Name of Supervisor
	Mo.	Yr.	Mo.	Yr.				
Abel Tool Co. 107-16 Rom Rd. Power City MA 01202 Telephone 413·349·2400	1	88	–	–	$200	$250	I want a Cooking job	Mr. Abel

Describe the work you did: Stamping Tools

II

Name and Address of Company and Type of Business	From		To		Weekly Starting Salary	Weekly Last Salary	Reason for Leaving	Name of Supervisor
	Mo.	Yr.	Mo.	Yr.				
M&P Machine Company 103 Bride Ave. Power City, MA 01202 Telephone 413·667·0900	7	86	12	87	$3.50/HR	$4.50/HR	I wanted more money	Oscar Garcia

Describe the work you did:

III

Name and Address of Company and Type of Business	From		To		Weekly Starting Salary	Weekly Last Salary	Reason for Leaving	Name of Supervisor
	Mo.	Yr.	Mo.	Yr.				
Telephone								

Describe the work you did:

IV

Name and Address of Company and Type of Business	From		To		Weekly Starting Salary	Weekly Last Salary	Reason for Leaving	Name of Supervisor
	Mo.	Yr.	Mo.	Yr.				
Telephone								

Describe the work you did:

If there is a particular employer(s), you do not wish us to contact, please indicate which one(s). #1, Mr. Abel because I have not told him I am leaving yet.

PERSONAL REFERENCES (Not Former Employers or Relatives)

Name and Occupation	Address	Phone Number
Henry Brod, Salesman	200 Tunnel Dr. Miami, FL 33172	(305) 592·6065
Minnie Herst, teacher	42 Elwill Dr. Stamford CT 06905	(203) 964·7021
Nick Turner, Carpenters Helper	786-10 Disk Dr. Power City MA 01202	(413) 806·2043

PLEASE READ AND SIGN BELOW

The facts set forth in my application for employment are true and complete. I understand that if employed, any false statement on this application may result in my dismissal. I further understand that this application is not and is not intended to be a contract of employment, nor does this application obligate the employer in any way if the employer decides to employ me. You are hereby authorized to make any investigation of my personal history and financial and credit record through any investigative or credit agencies or bureaus of your choice.

In making this application for employment I authorize you to make an investigative consumer report whereby information is obtained through personal interviews with my neighbors, friends, or others with whom I am acquainted. This inquiry, if made, may include information as to my character, general reputation, personal characteristics and mode of living. I understand that I have the right to make a written request within a reasonable period of time to receive additional, detailed information about the nature and scope of any such investigative report that is made.

Edward Pepper
Signature of Applicant

Getting a job is an important step in your life. Many forms have questions that you need to think about. Think about them first and then write your answers on the form.

1. Marital Status—The law says that you do not **have to** answer this question. You may, if you wish. You also do not have to answer questions about your religion, race, if you are male or female, or if you have a physical handicap. Of course, it is not a good idea to ask for a job if your physical handicap will stop you from doing that job.

2. Reason for Leaving—This part asks why you left your other job. Maybe you moved. You can write Family moved for the reason. Or maybe you had to take care of your sick mother. Then Had to stay home to take care of someone is the reason.
Did the company move or close down? Were many employees let go? Write Business closed or Business moved.
But, maybe you were fired. You don't want to say that you had a fight with another worker or your last boss. You don't want to lie, but you do want to look good. You may write Want more interesting job or Want better pay. Don't say bad things about your last boss or workers.

3. Rate of Pay Expected—How much money do you want for this job? Try to find out how much most people get for the job. You may not want to answer this on the form. Put a line there. Or write Open in that space. This means that you want to talk about the pay.

4. Last Salary—Write how much money you were making at your last job. If this will be your first job, put a line in this space.

5. References—Print names of people who will say good things about you. Don't give the names of relatives. You may give the name of a teacher or a storekeeper who knows you. Ask these people if you may use their names. Remember, the employer may call or write to your references.

Practice

You have been working in the stockroom of the Sticky Tape Company at 453 Liss Rd. in your city for two years. Mr. Cord is your boss. You have asked him for more money. Mr. Cord likes you, but he can't pay you more money.

Your friend, Frank Fink, works at the Burns Toaster Company at 171-32 Ash St. in your city. He told you about a job in the stockroom there. It pays $5 an hour. That is more money than you are making now.

You want to get a job at the Burns Toaster Co. Fill out the application form on page 27. Use your Information Sheet to help you.

Check Yourself

Look at your application form. Did you fill it out the right way? Let's see.

Answer these questions. Mark Yes or No.

	YES	NO
1. Did you print neatly?	☐	☐
2. Did you write in your Social Security Number?	☐	☐
3. Did you print Frank Fink after Referred by?	☐	☐
4. Did you write Sticky Tape Co. after Past Employment?	☐	☐
5. Did you write stockroom clerk after Position Desired?	☐	☐
6. Did you write $5/hour after Salary Desired?	☐	☐
7. Did you sign the form?	☐	☐

Most job application forms ask about your education and your past jobs. Think about the schools that you went to. Fill in the part of your Information Sheet about Education on page 5.

Have you had any jobs? Fill in the part of your Information Sheet about Jobs on page 6. Write your latest job first. What was your job before that? Write that one. Then keep going backwards.

What people will say good things about you? Fill in their names on your Information Sheet under Personal References.

BURNS TOASTER COMPANY, INC.
APPLICATION FOR EMPLOYMENT

PERSONAL INFORMATION

DATE _____   SOCIAL SECURITY NUMBER _____

NAME _____   AGE _____   SEX _____

LAST   FIRST   MIDDLE

PRESENT ADDRESS _____   PHONE NO. _____

STREET   CITY   STATE

DATE OF BIRTH _____   HEIGHT _____   WEIGHT _____   MARITAL STATUS _____

REFERRED BY

NAME _____   POSITION _____   PHONE # _____

POSITION DESIRED

POSITION _____   DATE YOU CAN START _____   SALARY DESIRED _____

EDUCATION

EDUCATION	NAME and LOCATION OF SCHOOL	YEARS ATTENDED	DATE GRADUATED
GRAMMAR SCHOOL			
HIGH SCHOOL			

MILITARY SERVICE RECORD

BRANCH _____   DATES OF DUTY — FROM-TO _____

RANK _____   DISCHARGE STATUS _____

PAST EMPLOYMENT   (LIST BELOW LAST 2 EMPLOYERS, STARTING WITH LAST ONE FIRST.)

DATE MONTH AND YEAR	NAME AND ADDRESS OF EMPLOYER	SALARY	POSITION	REASON FOR LEAVING
FROM				
TO				
FROM				
TO				

REFERENCES   GIVE THE NAMES OF THREE PERSONS NOT RELATED TO YOU, WHOM YOU HAVE KNOWN AT LEAST ONE YEAR.

	NAME	ADDRESS	BUSINESS	YEARS ACQUAINTED
1				
2				
3				

DATE _____   SIGNATURE _____

5   Money Orders

Many ads on T.V. and in magazines tell about things to buy. If you have a checking account, you can use checks to send for these things. You pay by sending a check. Never send **cash** in the mail. It is not safe.

But you may not have a checking account. You can send a money order in the mail. You can buy money orders at banks or at the post office. Money orders are safe to send in the mail.

The post office will stamp the amount of your money order on the form. Then you must fill in the rest. Fill it in right away. Anyone can cash a blank money order.

After <u>Pay to</u>, write the name of the person or company that you are paying. Then fill in the address of this person or company. Now only this person or company can cash this money order.

After <u>From</u>, write your name and address. You are now ready to mail your money order.

Important Words
Cash—money in coins and bills.
Receipt—paper that shows that you have paid for something.
Shipping and handling—the cost of sending things in the mail; this is sometimes called postage and handling.
Refund—you get your money back.
Satisfaction guaranteed—you can get your money back if you are not happy with what you bought.

Nick's sister just had a baby girl. Nick saw an ad for birth announcements in a magazine. He showed the ad to his sister. She asked Nick to order the cards.

Nick does not have a checking account yet. He knows that he must not send cash in the mail. So he went to the post office to buy a money order.

A money order costs 75¢ at the post office. Nick needed a money order for $3.00. So he paid a total of $3.75.

Look at Nick's money order below. He wrote <u>New Kid Cards, Inc.</u> after <u>Pay to</u> because New Kid Cards will get the $3. Only New Kid Cards will be able to cash this money order. He filled in the address for New Kid Cards. Then he wrote his own name and address after <u>From</u> because he is sending the money order. He tore the **receipt** from the money order and saved it.

Nick's money order

Receipt for Nick's money order

Nick filled out the form in the ad. He wanted two sets of cards. He wrote 2 in the space before set(s). He wrote 3.00 in the space after the dollar sign because he is sending $3.00. Then he wrote his name and address on the form. He put an X next to Girl so he will get the right kind of cards.

Mail To:
New Kid Cards, Inc.
P.O. Box 10B
Stork, PA 19747

Please send me 2 set(s) of 10 cards and envelopes at $1.50 per set. Enclosed is my check or money order (no cash, please) for $ 3.00 payable to New Kid Cards, Inc. My birth announcement is for a ☐ BOY ☒ GIRL.

Name *Nick Turner*
Address *786-10 Disk Drive*
City *Power City*
State *MA* Zip *01202*

Ad for birth announcement cards

Nick sent the money order and the form in a stamped and addressed envelope. Two weeks later the cards came in the mail. His sister was very happy.

Some ads do not a have form. You may have to write a short business letter to buy things from these ads. Send your letter with your money order. Remember to keep your receipt from your money order and keep a copy of your letter.

NOTE: Look at Chapter 10, How to Write Right 1 for help in writing a business letter.

Look at this ad. Send to Stuck Labels, Inc. for 50 one-line labels. It will cost $3.95 for the name labels and $1.25 for shipping. That is a total of $5.20.

Fill in the money order and the form in the ad. Remember to tell Stuck Labels, Inc. what name you want printed on your labels.

IRON-ON LABELS

Keep clothes out of the LOST & FOUND
YOUR NAME in bold, blue letters printed on sturdy PRE-CUT cloth labels 2″ × 3/8″. Will adhere to any fabric, won't fade, rub or wash off. No need to sew. Irons on quickly and easily for permanent I.D. Ideal for school, camp, uniforms, nursing homes, church, gym, play groups.
**All orders mailed FIRST CLASS
for immediate delivery.**
Satisfaction Guaranteed or your Money Back
For 50 one-line labels, send $3.95
For 100 one-line labels, send $4.95
STUCK LABELS, INC.
P.O. Box 5, Jacksonville, FL 32265

Please send me:

___150 one-line labels @ $3.95

___100 one-line labels @ $4.95

Add $1.25 for shipping & handling

Name on label should be:

_____

Ship to:

Name_____

Address _____

City _____State_____Zip_____

BANK MONEY ORDER 121966

$\frac{53\text{-}107}{113}$

PAY TO THE ORDER OF _____ 19 __

$ _____

5 DLS **20** CTS **DOLLARS**

NOT VALID OVER $500.00

_____
NAME

_____
ADDRESS

⑈121966⑈ ⑆011301073⑊ ⑈03 200 019⑈

Check Yourself

Look at your ad form and money order again. Did you write them right? Let's see.

Answer these questions. Mark Yes or No. YES ✔ NO

1. Did you write <u>Stuck Labels, Inc.</u> after <u>Pay to the order of</u> on the money order? ☐ ☐

2. Did you write your name and address on the money order? ☐ ☐

3. Does your form show how many labels you are ordering? ☐ ☐

6   Banking Forms

Important Words

Service charges—money that you pay the bank to keep a checking account.
Joint account—one account for two or more persons.
Account title—your name; in a joint account it is all the names on the account.
Deposit—to put money into a bank; the money that you put into a bank.
Balance—how much money you have left in your bank account.
Bank statement—what the bank sends you every month. It tells all about your checking account for the last month.
Endorse—to sign your name.
Total—to add up; the whole amount.
Teller—the clerk at the bank window. This person handles your money.
Acc't—a short way to write account.

Banks help us in many ways. It is safer to keep money at a bank than at home. So many people have bank accounts. You can put your money in the bank or take it out at any time.

There are many kinds of bank accounts. There are savings accounts and checking accounts. Sometimes, banks pay us for keeping our money in the bank. Sometimes, we must pay the bank for keeping our money in the bank. We may have to pay a little money every month for an account. This money is called a **service charge** or fee. There may be charges for ordering checkbooks and for every check that we write.

Every bank has its own rules. Different banks have different fees for checking accounts. Rules are always changing. Talk to the clerks at two or more banks. Then think about your needs. Then pick the best bank for you.

People with checking accounts can pay their bills with checks. You can pay your rent by check. Just mail it to your landlord. You can pay your telephone bill by check. Mail it to the telephone company.

You will save time because you won't have to pay these bills in person. And you won't have to walk around with lots of cash.

Someone at the bank will help you open your account. You will have to show some identification. You may show your birth certificate, driver's license, or other kind of photo identification.

Bank Signature Card

Only you can sign your checks. So the bank has to know what your signature looks like. You will have to fill out a bank signature card. The bank will keep this card.

Nick wanted to open a checking account. He talked to a worker at the bank. The bank clerk gave him a form for a bank signature card.

Nick read the card. He left the gray part blank. The bank will fill that in.

Below the number 1, he printed his name. On the next line, he signed his name next to the X. He wrote in his Social Security number in the boxes under Soc. Sec. No.

Some bank accounts are for more than one person. These accounts are called **joint accounts**. Both people on a joint account can put money in and take money out of the account. Nick did not want his account to be a joint account. So he did not fill in the spaces below the number 2.

He printed Nick Evan Turner as the **Account Title**. This is the name that will be on his checks. Then he filled in his telephone number, address, and birth date.

Nick had to make a **deposit** into his new account. He gave $50 to the bank clerk. This money will open his account.

Later, the bank will send him checkbooks. Each check will have Nick's name, address, and account number printed on it.

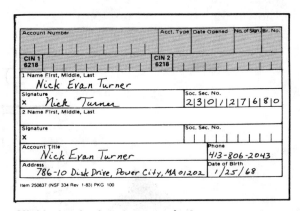

Nick's bank signature card

Practice

You are opening a bank account for yourself. Fill in the bank signature card on page 35. Use your own Social Security number or 123-45-6789.

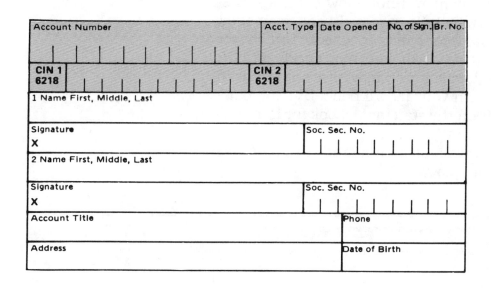

Account Number		Acct. Type	Date Opened	No. of Sign.	Br. No.

CIN 1 6218	CIN 2 6218

1 Name First, Middle, Last

Signature	Soc. Sec. No.
X	

2 Name First, Middle, Last

Signature	Soc. Sec. No.
X	

Account Title	Phone

Address	Date of Birth

Look at your bank signature card again. Did you fill in all the parts? If not, go back and write it right.

$ _____ _____ 19 _____

1727

Tax Item [ ]

To _____

_____

BAL. FWD.		
AMT. DEPOSITED		
TOTAL		
AMT. THIS CHECK		
BALANCE		
MISCELLANEOUS DEDUCTION		
BAL. CAR'D. FWD.		

Stub from a checkbook

People with checking accounts must always have information about the money in their account. They need to know their balance. The **balance** is the amount of money in the account.

The balance gets bigger when you put money into your account. It gets smaller when you take money out of your account. No one can remember all the changes in the balance. So you have to write it down each time it changes.

Some checkbooks have stubs on every check. Other checkbooks have record books. Stubs and record books help you to know your balance.

Every time you make a deposit or write a check, write it down. Write it on your stub or in your record book. Don't wait until later! Add when you make deposits. Subtract when you write checks.

Every month the bank will send your used checks and a **bank statement**. The statement shows all your deposits for the last month. It also shows the checks that you wrote. It tells the balance in your account on the day of the statement.

But your records will **not** always be the same as the bank's. Here's why.

The bank statement will show fees and service charges. You must subtract them from the balance in your records.

The bank statement will not show checks if they have not been cashed. Your record book may show that you have paid your rent by check. But maybe your landlord did not cash your rent check yet. The landlord may still have it. You may have subtracted it from the balance in your record book. But the bank does not show it on the statement. Look for it in your statement next month.

Keep your bank statements and used checks together in a safe place.

ENTER ALL TRANSACTIONS THAT AFFECT YOUR ACCOUNT BALANCE			DEBITS			CREDITS	BALANCE	
ITEM NO. OR CODE	DATE	DESCRIPTION OF TRANSACTION	(−) PAYMENT OR WITHDRAWAL	√ T	(−) FEE	(+) DEPOSIT OR INTEREST		

BE SURE TO RECORD AUTOMATIC PAYMENTS / DEPOSITS ON DATE AUTHORIZED.

Page from a record book

Deposit Slips

Fill out a deposit slip when you put money into your account. Get checking account deposit slips at the bank. Fill out the date, your name, your account number, and the amount of your deposit.

Your bank may send you deposit slips with your name and account number on them. On these deposit slips, you have to fill in only the date and the amount of the deposit.

Then you will have to write three things on the back of your check.
1. The words For deposit only
2. Your account number
3. Your signature. This is what **endorse** means.

Be careful! An endorsed check can be cashed by anyone. Always endorse your checks at the bank. It is safe that way.

Look at Vera's deposit slip for her checking account. Her name and account number are printed on the deposit slip.

Vera wanted to deposit her paycheck for $175.00 into her checking account. First, she filled in the date.

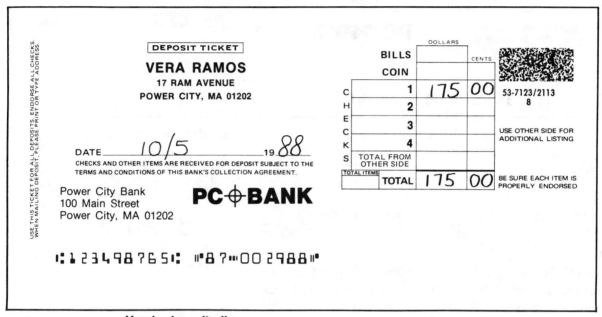

Vera's deposit slip

The back of Vera's check

Vera did not deposit any cash. She left that line blank.

She filled in the part next to the number 1. This part is for depositing checks. Vera wrote 175 to the left of the line and 00 to the right of the line. Then she wrote 175 00 next to Total at the bottom.

Vera was almost ready to deposit her paycheck. First, she wrote the words For deposit only on the back of the check. Then she wrote her account number. Then she endorsed her check.

Vera gave her deposit slip and her check to the **teller**. The teller gave her back one part of the deposit form. It is a receipt. It proves that Vera made a deposit of $175.00 on October 5, 1988. Vera saved the receipt.

Ed Pepper made a deposit into his checking account. He deposited $45.00 in cash and two checks. One check was for $175.80 and the other was for $60.00.

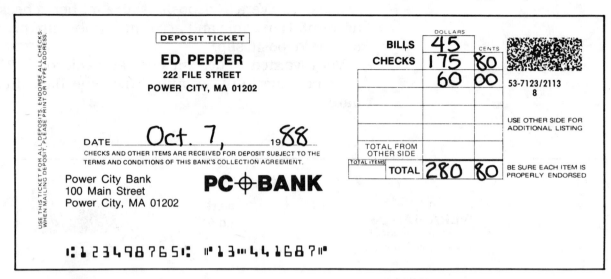

Ed's deposit slip

Ed wrote <u>45</u> in the <u>Bills</u> space. In the <u>Checks</u> spaces he wrote <u>175 80</u> on the first line and <u>60 00</u> on the next line.

He added it all together and filled in <u>280 80</u> in the <u>Total</u> space at the bottom. He remembered to fill out the back of each check and endorse it.

> *For deposit only*
> *13-441687*
> *Ed Pepper*

The back of Ed's check

Practice

You are depositing $5 in cash and three checks. One check is for $10.00, one is for $35.00, and one is for $50. Fill out the deposit slip below.

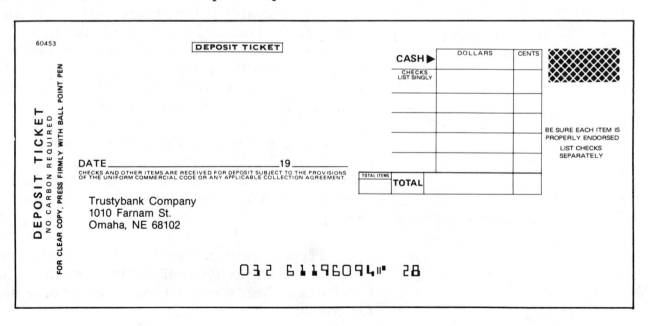

Look at your deposit slip again. Does your deposit total $100.00? If not, go back and write it right.

Checks

If you have a checking account, you can write checks to pay bills or to take money out of your checking account. You write six things on each check.

1. The date that you are writing the check.
2. The person or company that you are paying
3. The amount of the check in numbers only
4. The amount of the check in words and in numbers
5. Your signature
6. A note that tells you why you wrote the check

Each of these six things is important. But the most important one is your signature. The bank will not cash a check that is not signed.

Vera is paying her telephone bill with a check from her own checking account. Her name and address are already on the check. Her account number is printed on the bottom of the check. She will send this check to the Power City Telephone Company.

```
VERA RAMOS                                          5098
17 RAM AVENUE
POWER CITY, MA 01202         Oct 10  19 88        1-8/210
                                                  Branch 32

PAY TO THE   Power City Tel. Co.              $ 35 25/100
ORDER OF

Thirty-five and 25/100 ————————————————— DOLLARS

Power City Bank        PC⬦BANK
100 Main Street
Power City, MA 01202
                                      Vera Ramos
FOR September telephone bill

⑈123498765⑈ ⑈87⑈002988⑈   5098
```

Vera's check to the telephone company

Vera filled in the date. After the words Pay to the order of, she wrote Power City Tel. Co. Then she wrote the amount of money in numbers. Next to the dollar sign, she wrote 35 25/100.

At the beginning of the next line, she wrote Thirty-five and $^{25}/_{100}$ in words and numbers. Then she drew a line from the end of her writing to the end of the line. Now no one can write another word in this space. No one can easily change the amount of Vera's check.

The word dollars is already printed at the end of the line. So Vera did not need to write the word dollars.

Vera signed the check on the bottom line on the right.

She wanted to remember what this check was for. She wrote September telephone bill next to For.

Vera was not depositing money into her own account. She was paying someone else by check. So she did not endorse the back of this check. The telephone company will endorse the check when they deposit it into their bank account. Then Vera's bank will give the telephone company's bank the money.

<table>
<tr><td colspan="2">FRACTIONS FOR AMOUNTS UNDER $1</td></tr>
<tr><td>$^{00}/_{100}$</td><td>means no cents</td></tr>
<tr><td>$^{09}/_{100}$</td><td>means 9 cents</td></tr>
<tr><td>$^{25}/_{100}$</td><td>means 25 cents</td></tr>
<tr><td>$^{79}/_{100}$</td><td>means 79 cents</td></tr>
</table>

Practice

Formal Ike wants you to lend him $50.50. Write a check to him. Fill in all the parts and sign your own name.

```
                                                       1727

                                          _____19_____  1-30/210

PAY TO THE
ORDER OF_____  $

_____DOLLARS

      WE TRUST



FOR_____         _____
  ⑆987651234⑆  ⑈12345⑈55432⑈    1727
```

Look at your check to Ike again. Is it right? If not, go back and write it right.

When you want to take money out of your own checking account, write a check to yourself. You can do it in two ways. After Pay to the order of, you can write your name or you can write Cash. You must endorse a check to yourself, but you do **not** write For deposit only.

Remember, you must have money in your bank account to take money out.

Ed Pepper needed $40.00 in cash from his checking account. He wrote a check to himself. Look at Ed's check. He filled it out the right way.

ED PEPPER
222 FILE STREET
POWER CITY, MA 01202

5099

Oct. 12 19 88   1-8/210
Branch 32

PAY TO THE ORDER OF _Ed Pepper_ $ 40 00/100

Forty and 00/100 _____ DOLLARS

Power City Bank
100 Main Street
Power City, MA 01202

PC⊕BANK

FOR _Cash_   _Ed Pepper_

⑆123498765⑆ ⑈13⑉441687⑊ 5099

Ed's check to himself

Ed took his check to his bank. He endorsed the back at the bank. The teller gave him $40 in cash.

Practice

You have a checking account. Today you need $32.00 in cash. Use the check below and write a check to yourself. Your account number is on the check. Endorse the back.

5100

_____ 19_____   1-8/210
Branch 32

PAY TO THE ORDER OF _____ $

_____ DOLLARS

Piggy Bank and Trust Co.

FOR _____   _____

⑆987651234⑆ ⑈12345⑉55432⑊ 5100

Here is the back of your check. Sign it the right way.

Check Yourself

Answer these questions. Mark Yes or No.

	YES	NO
1. Did you write today's date on the check?	□	□
2. Did you write your name or Cash after Pay to the Order of?	□	□
3. Did you write the amount in two places on the check?	□	□
4. Did you draw a line after the amount in words and numbers?	□	□
5. Did you sign your name on the bottom line of the check?	□	□
6. Did you endorse the back of the check?	□	□
7. Did you write For deposit only on the back of the check?	□	□
8. Did you write your account number on the back of your check?	□	□

If you have a bank account, fill in the part of your Information Sheet about bank accounts on page 5.

7 Voter Registration Form

Important Words
Register—to sign up for.
Naturalization papers—papers that show that you have become a citizen.
Residence—where you live.
Enroll—to join.
Permanent—for a long time; forever.
Former—past.
Certificate—a paper that proves that you did or finished something.
Optional—something that you can do or not do.
Procure—to get.
Felony—a crime.

In the United States, the president and other people in the government run our country. We pick our leaders by voting for them in elections. Only American citizens may vote.

New voters must **register** to vote in an election. You can get a registration form at the Board of Elections. Look in the back of your telephone book. Look for Government offices, State, City, or County. You will see Elections, Bd. of. Call that telephone number and ask them to send you a registration form. Tell them your name and address.

If you skip voting a few times, you must fill out a voter registration form again. When you move to another city or state, you must fill out a new registration form.

Maybe you are a citizen, but you were not born in this country. The information on your **naturalization papers** will help you to fill out this registration form.

Each state has its own voter registration form. The questions are a little different on the forms from different states.

Vera Ramos lives in Massachusetts. She wanted to register to vote. She went to the nearest Board of Elections for a registration form. In Massachusetts, the voter registration form is called an Affidavit of Registration. An affidavit is a kind of form. On this form Vera will have to sign her name to show that she is telling the truth. If she does not tell the truth it is a crime.

Vera printed her name on the form. She wrote her last name first because the form says Last Name, First Name, Initial.

On the next line, she wrote the number of her house under House No. Then she wrote Ram Ave. under Street Name. She put Power City under City and 01202 under Zip Code.

On January 1, 1988 Vera was living at 205 North Media Dr., Power City 01202. So she wrote this address on the next line. Vera drew a line in the next space because she has not moved from a different town or city.

Vera drew a line in the next space because she has not changed her name.

Then she filled in her date of birth. She wrote Power City, MA USA as her place of birth.

Only U.S. Citizens are allowed to vote in elections. Vera is a citizen because she was born in the United States. So she checked Birth.

Vera works in an office. She is a secretary, so she wrote Secretary on the line under Occupation.

Vera filled out the form on October 14. She wrote that date in the space at the bottom of the form.

Vera read the last paragraph. This paragraph asks her to make sure that everything she has written is the truth. She was telling the truth on this form and she has never broken any laws about elections.

Vera took the form to the clerk and signed it. The clerk watched Vera sign the form, so the clerk was Vera's witness. Then the clerk signed the form in the space for Witness.

Soon Vera will be able to vote.

The Commonwealth of Massachusetts

Department of the State Secretary

AFFIDAVIT OF REGISTRATION

DECLARACION JURADA DE INSCRIPCION

Michael Joseph Connolly

Secretary of State

PRINT ALL INFORMATION - USE LETRA DE MOLDE

LAST NAME - APELLIDO	FIRST NAME - PRIMER NOMBRE	INITIAL - INICIAL
Ramos	Vera	

HOUSE NO. - CASA NO.	STREET NAME - CALLE	CITY - CIUDAD	ZIP CODE
17	Ram Ave	Power City	01202

RESIDENCE JAN. 1 (IF DIFFERENT FROM ABOVE) - RESIDENCIA ENERO 1 (SI ES DIFERENTE A LA DE ARRIBA)

205 North Media Dr.   Power City   01202

LAST PREVIOUS RESIDENCE IN ANOTHER CITY OR TOWN, IF ANY - DIRECCION ANTERIOR A LA PRESENTE EN OTRA CIUDAD O PUEBLO

NAME USED AT THIS RESIDENCE (IF DIFFERENT FROM ABOVE) - NOMBRE QUE USO EN ESA RESIDENCIA (SI ES DIFERENTE AL DE ARRIBA)

DATE OF BIRTH - FECHA DE NACIMIENTO			PLACE OF BIRTH - LUGAR DE NACIMIENTO			U.S. CITIZENSHIP - CIUDADANIA DE E.U.	
MONTH - MES	DAY - DIA	YEAR - AÑO	CITY - CIUDAD	STATE - ESTADO	COUNTRY - PAIS	BIRTH NACIMIENTO	NATURALIZED NATURALIZADO
2	11	68	Power City	MA	USA	✓	

OCCUPATION - OCUPACION	DO YOU WISH TO ENROLL IN A POLITICAL PARTY? - ¿DESEA INSCRIBIRSE EN ALGUN PARTIDO POLITICO?		
Secretary	DEMOCRATIC DEMOCRATA ☐	REPUBLICAN REPUBLICANO ☐	NO NO ✓

I HEREBY SWEAR (AFFIRM) THAT I AM THE PERSON NAMED ABOVE, THAT THE ABOVE INFORMATION IS TRUE, THAT I AM A CITIZEN OF THE UNITED STATES, THAT I AM NOT A PERSON UNDER GUARDIANSHIP, THAT I AM NOT TEMPORARILY OR PERMANENTLY DISQUALIFIED BY LAW FROM VOTING BECAUSE OF CORRUPT PRACTICES IN RESPECT TO ELECTIONS, AND THAT I CONSIDER THIS RESIDENCE TO BE MY HOME. SIGNED UNDER THE PAINS AND PENALTIES OF PERJURY.

YO JURO (AFIRMO) QUE SOY LA PERSONA NOMBRADA ARRIBA, QUE LA INFORMACION ARRIBA INDICADA ES VERDADERA, QUE SOY CIUDADANO DE LOS ESTADOS UNIDOS, QUE NO SOY PERSONA BAJO TUTELA, QUE ANTE LA LEY NO ESTOY DESCALIFICADO TEMPORALMENTE O PERMANENTEMENTE PARA VOTAR POR RAZONES DE PRACTICAS CORRUPTAS RELACIONADAS CON LAS ELECCIONES, Y QUE CONSIDERO ESTA RESIDENCIA MI HOGAR.

FIRMADO BAJO PENA Y PENALIDADES DE PERJURIO

Vera Ramos

SIGNATURE OF REGISTRANT   FIRMA DEL SUSCRITO

WITNESS TESTIGO   John Hannah   REGISTRAR - REGISTRADOR

DATE FECHA   10-14-88

50M-9/84-800291

Vera's voter registration form

Practice

Fill out this voter registration form for yourself. Sign your own name.

VOTER REGISTRATION APPLICATION	OFFICIAL USE ONLY

VOTER REGISTRATION APPLICATION
(SOLICITUD PARA REGISTRO DE VOTANTE)
(Articles 5.13a and 5.13b , Vernon's Texas Election Code)
PLEASE COMPLETE ALL OF THE INFORMATION BELOW. PRINT IN INK OR TYPE.
(POR FAVOR COMPLETE LA INFORMACION SIGUIENTE. ESCRIBA EN LETRA DE MOLDE CON TINTA O ESCRIBA A MAQUINA)

OFFICIAL USE ONLY
(SOLAMENTE PARA USO OFICIAL)

CERTIFICATE NUMBER	APPLICATION NUMBER
PCT	EDR

LAST NAME *(APELLIDO)*	FIRST NAME (NOT HUSBAND'S) *(NOMBRE – NO DEL ESPOSO)*	MIDDLE NAME *(SEGUNDO NOMBRE)*	MAIDEN NAME *(APELLIDO DE SOLTERA)*

SEX *(SEXO)*	DATE OF BIRTH *(FECHA DE NACIMIENTO)* MONTH DAY YEAR *(MES) (DIA) (AÑO)*	PLACE OF BIRTH *(LUGAR DE NACIMIENTO)* CITY OR COUNTY *(CIUDAD O CONDADO)*	STATE OR FOREIGN COUNTRY *(ESTADO O PAIS EXTRANJERO)*	IF YOU ARE A NATURALIZED CITIZEN, INDICATE THE COURT OF NATURALIZATION OR ITS LOCATION: *(SI ES CIUDADANO NATURALIZADO INDIQUE LA CORTE DE NATURALIZACION O SU LOCALIDAD)*

PERMANENT RESIDENCE ADDRESS: STREET ADDRESS AND APARTMENT NUMBER; IF NONE,
DESCRIBE LOCATION OF RESIDENCE:
(DIRECCION DE RESIDENCIA PERMANENTE: Calle y numero de departamento, si no tiene, debe dar una descripcion de la localidad.)

IF MAIL CANNOT BE DELIVERED TO PERMANENT RESIDENCE ADDRESS, PROVIDE MAILING ADDRESS:
(EN CASO DE QUE EL CORREO NO PUEDA SER ENTREGADO A SU RESIDENCIA PERMANENTE, DEBE DAR OTRA DIRECCION PARA ENTRIEGO)

CITY, STATE, and ZIP:
(CIUDAD, ESTADO Y ZONA POSTAL)

IF YOU ARE NOW REGISTERED IN ANOTHER TEXAS COUNTY, COMPLETE THE FOLLOWING: *(SI ESTAS REGISTRADO EN OTRO CONDADO DE TEJAS COMPLETE LO SIGUIENTE:)* COUNTY OF FORMER RESIDENCE: *(Condado de residencia previa:)*	RESIDENCE ADDRESS AS SHOWN ON CERTIFICATE IN THAT COUNTY: *(Dirección de residencia mostrada en el certificado de ese condado.)*	IF YOU WERE REGISTERED BUT DID NOT RECEIVE A NEW CERTIFICATE, COMPLETE THE FOLLOWING: *(SI ESTABA REGISTRADO PERO NO RECIBIO SU CERTIFICADO NUEVO COMPLETE LO SIGUIENTE:)* COUNTY OF PREVIOUS REGISTRATION: *(Condado de registro previo:)*	RESIDENCE ADDRESS AS SHOWN ON PREVIOUS CERTIFICATE: *(Dirección de residencia mostrada en su certificado previo:)*

*SOCIAL SECURITY NUMBER *(NUMERO DE SEGURO SOCIAL)*	TELEPHONE NUMBER (OPTIONAL) *(TELEFONO) (OPCIONAL)*	CURRENT PRECINCT NUMBER OR NAME, IF KNOWN: (OPTIONAL) *(NUMERO DE PRECINTO O EL NOMBRE DEL SITIO) (OPCIONAL)*

THE APPLICANT IS A CITIZEN OF THE UNITED STATES AND A RESIDENT OF THIS COUNTY. I CERTIFY THAT THE INFORMATION PROVIDED IS CORRECT. I UNDERSTAND THAT THE GIVING OF FALSE INFORMATION TO PROCURE THE REGISTRATION OF A VOTER IS A FELONY.
(El solicitant, es ciudadano estadounidense y residente de este condado. Afirmo que la información proporcionada es verdadera. Comprendo que es una felonia de proporcionar información falsa para tratar registración de votante.)

X _____
SIGNATURE OF APPLICANT (OR AGENT)
(FIRMA DE SOLICITANTE O AGENTE)

FOR AGENT:
(PARA AGENTE:)
Application may be by agent who must be a qualified voter of this county and must be the applicant's husband, wife, father, mother, son, or daughter.
(La solicitud puede efectuarse con la ayuda de un votante calificado en el condado que sea uno de los siguientes: esposo, esposa, padre, madre, hijo, o hija.)
I AM THE _____ OF THE APPLICANT.
(Yo soy el/la) **(relationship)** *(relacción)* *(del solicitante)*

FOR WITNESS:
(PARA TESTIGO)
If the applicant is unable to sign his name, he shall make his mark in the presence of a witness. If the applicant is unable to make his mark, the witness shall state that fact on the application.
(Si el solicitante no puede firmar su nombre, debe hacer su marca en la presencia de un testigo. Si el solicitante no puede hacer su marca, el testigo debe declarar la razon sobre la solicitud.)
Signature and address of witness:
(Firma y dirección del testigo:)

*The disclosure of social security number is voluntary. It is solicited by authority of Article 5.13b, V.T.E.C. and will be used only to maintain the accuracy of the registration records.
(La revelación de su numero de seguro social es totalmente voluntario. Su numero es solicitado por autoridad de Articulo 5.13b, V.T.E.C., y sera utilizado unicamente para preservar la exactitud de los archivos de registro.)

Check Yourself

Look at your voter registration form again. Did you write it right? Let's see.

Answer these questions. Mark Yes or No.

	YES ✔	NO
1. Did you print your last name first?	☐	☐
2. Did you write the month, day, and year of your birth in numbers?	☐	☐
3. Did you write your whole address?	☐	☐
4. Did you sign your name next to the X?	☐	☐

8 Driver's License Application Form

Important Words

Examiner—someone who tests you.
Requirement—something that you need before you can do something.
Residential address—where you live.
Operate—to drive.
Suspended or revoked—taken away.
Restored—given back.
Presently—now.
Exactly—just like something else.
Amend—to change.
Former name—your name as you used to write it.
Restriction—limit on something.
Consent—to say yes.
Guardian—someone who takes care of you; not a parent.
Duplicate—a copy.
Renewal—bringing a license up to date.
Original license—the first one.
Reciprocity license—a license given in one state because you already have a license from another state.
Hearing impairment—something wrong with your hearing.
Physical disability—something wrong with your body.
Expiration date—the last day that something is good.

Some day you may be the happy owner of a car. But you need a license to drive it. Even if you don't own a car, a driver's license is important. You need a license to drive someone else's car. You can use your license for identification and to prove your age.

Most state laws say that you must be 18 years old to get a driver's license. Some states let you have a license sooner than that.

First you may need a Learner's Permit or Instruction Permit to practice driving on the road. All states let you start learning to drive before you are 18 years old. There must be a licensed driver in the car with you. Each state has its own laws about driver's permits and licenses. Find out about the laws in your state.

Get a driver's license application form at the Motor Vehicle Bureau or the Department of Motor Vehicles in your city or town. Every state has different forms.

In all states, you must pass three tests to get your driver's license.

1. A written test. This will show if you know the driving laws. The Motor Vehicle Bureau will give you a small book to study for this test.
2. An eye test. This will show if your eyes are good for driving. You can wear glasses for this test.
3. A road test. This will show if you can drive a car. An **examiner** will sit next to you and you will drive.

If you do not pass these tests, you may take them again.

Nick Turner lives in Massachusetts. He wants to get his driver's license. He got his permit and has learned how to drive.

Look at how Nick filled out the front of his application for a driver's license. He only filled out the part on the right side. The examiner will fill out the parts on the left later.

Nick read the first question. He had to look in the Massachusetts driver's book to answer it. The book told him that Class 3 is for a regular license. So Nick checked Class 3. Then he wrote his name and address in parts 2 and 3. He did not fill in number 4 because his mailing address is not different from his home address. He put a line in that part.

In part 5, Nick wrote out his date of birth. In parts 6 and 7, he filled in his height and the word male. Nick did not take a driving class in school, so he does not have a Massachusetts driver's education certificate. He drew a line in that space. In number 9, Nick wrote in his Social Security number.

LICENSE APPLICATION

REGISTRY OF MOTOR VEHICLES
100 NASHUA STREET
BOSTON, MASS. 02114

REPORT with this application for examination

AT		DATE	TIME
			Clerk

Requirement: a birth, baptismal or school certificate or other satisfactory evidence of age

Applicant must type or print in ink answers to questions 1 through 16

DATE EXAM'D	PASS		FAIL

FEE REC'D	RET'D	EXAMINER	BADGE

VISION	Right	Left	Both	Result
Without Glasses	20	20	20	
With Glasses	20	20	20	
FIELD				
COLOR	Red	Green	Yellow	

Written Test		
Road Test	CLASS	
Vehicle Used		
Registration Number		
Sponsor		
Sponsor License Number		
Removal		
Restriction		

CHECK ONLY ONE BLOCK (REFER TO DRIVERS' MANUAL FOR CLASS INFORMATION)

1. CLASS 1 ☐   CLASS 2 ☐   CLASS 3 ☑   MOTORCYCLE ☐

2. Name ... *Nick*   *E.*   *Turner* ...
   First Name   Middle Initial   Last Name

3. Mail Address No. *786-10 Disk Drive* .... St
   (If post office box, residential address must be shown.)
   Power City   *MA*   *01202*
   City or Town   State   Zip Code

4. Residential Address No. _____ St
   (IF DIFFERENT FROM MAIL ADDRESS ABOVE)
   _____
   City or Town   State   Zip Code

5. Date of Birth: month *January* ...... day *25* ...... year *1968*

6. Height ...... *5* ... ft. ...... *11* ... in.   7. Sex *Male*

8. Massachusetts Driver Education Certificate Number ....

9. Social Security Number ... *230 12 7680* ....

DO NOT WRITE IN THIS SPACE

You will not be examined if you are late. Appointment fee $5.00 to be filed with application at nearest Registry office

(OVER)

The front of Nick's driver's license application

Now look at the back of the same form. For question <u>10</u>, Nick wrote <u>Yes</u> because he has his Learner's Permit. Nick has never had a license before, so he wrote <u>No</u> for question <u>11</u>. He has never been in trouble with the law, so he wrote <u>No</u> for questions <u>12</u> and <u>13</u>.

Nick doesn't have any physical disabilities and is in good health. He answered <u>No</u> for questions <u>14</u>, <u>15</u> and <u>16</u>.

Nick read the part after question <u>16</u>. He did not understand all of it so he asked someone for help. Then he signed the form.

---

10. Have you ever been issued a Learner's Permit in Massachusetts? (Answer "yes" or "no")   *Yes*
    Date *June, 1988*   Where issued? *Power City*

11. Have you ever had a license to operate   Date
    in Massachusetts or any other state?   *No*   Where?   of Exp.
    Has it ever been suspended or revoked?
    If yes, why?   Has it been restored?

12. If unlicensed in Massachusetts, has your RIGHT to operate ever
    been suspended here or in any other state? (Answer "yes" or "no")   *No*
    Has it been restored?

13. Have you been convicted of any crime or adjudged a delinquent child within the last ten years? Do not
    include parking violations. (Answer "yes" or "no")   *No*
    If "yes," for what reason?

14. Have you any physical disability that may prevent safe operation of a motor vehicle?   *No*
    If so, explain

15. Have you been treated within the last five years for
    A. Any heart disorder? (Answer "yes" or "no")   *No*   D. Drug Dependency? (Answer "yes" or "no")   *No*
    B. Epilepsy or fainting spells? (Answer "yes" or "no")   *No*   E. Mental Illness? (Answer "yes" or "no")   *No*
    C. Alcoholism? (Answer "yes" or "no")   *No*

16. Are you currently taking medication for a mental, nervous or physical disorder? (Answer "yes" or "no")   *No*

I, the undersigned, hereby apply for a license to operate motor vehicles and state that the statements herein are true to the best of my knowledge and belief.
In case the license herein applied for is issued, I hereby irrevocably appoint the Registrar of Motor Vehicles or his successor in office my attorney upon whom process against me may be served as provided in the General Laws and agree that process so served, if I am notified of such service as provided therein, shall be of the same legal effect as if served on me personally and that the mailing by the Registrar of a copy thereof to me at my last address as appearing on the Registrar's records shall be sufficient notice to me of such service. (G.L., Ch.90)

Signature must be full and legible (Write) ..... *Nick* .... *E.* .... *Turner*
                                                    First Name   Middle Initial   Last Name

FALSE STATEMENTS ARE PUNISHABLE BY FINE, IMPRISONMENT OR BOTH (Gen. Laws, Ch. 90, Sec.24)

PARENTAL CONSENT To be filled out by the parent, guardian, or person standing in place of parent of the above applicant.
TO THE REGISTRAR: I hereby certify that I am a (Check One)   (False statements made under penalties of perjury.)
parent ....., guardian ....., person standing in place of parent ......,of the above-named applicant who is less than 18 years of age but not less than 16½ years of age, and that my consent is given as required by G. L., Chap. 90, Section 8 that said applicant may be granted a license to operate motor vehicles.

(Write) NAME .... ADDRESS

I examined and hereby certify the above named applicant passed the prescribed examination.
FORM E-2. 300M-10/84-801521   Signature of Examiner ....   Badge #

REGISTRY USE ONLY
FIN. TR. NO.
EXAM FEE
FIN. TR. NO.
LICENSE FEE

The back of Nick's driver's license application

Many forms have a short paragraph before the space for your signature. Always read this paragraph before you sign the form. Many times, this part of a form is hard to read. Many people have trouble with it. Ask for help if you do not understand it.

Practice

You do not have a driver's license yet. You want to get one. Fill out this application for a driver's license.

R-229 REV. 11-85

VOID UNLESS VALIDATED BELOW
↓

DMV USE ONLY	☐ NEW	☐ CHANGE OF TYPE	☐ MOTORCYCLE	☐ OTHER

APPLICATION FOR CONNECTICUT DRIVER'S LICENSE

INSTRUCTIONS: Complete questions 1 through 23. Please print clearly.
After completing questions, read and follow
"IMPORTANT" instructions located after question 23.

STATE OF CONNECTICUT
DEPARTMENT OF MOTOR VEHICLES

1. APPLICANT'S NAME (Last, First, Middle Initial)	2. SEX	3. AGE	4. DATE OF BIRTH	5. HEIGHT	6. COLOR OF EYES
				ft. in.	

7. MAILING ADDRESS (No., Street, City or Town, Zip Code)	8. RESIDENCE ADDRESS (If different)

9. BIRTHPLACE (Include country if foreign born)	10. U.S. CITIZEN? ☐ YES ☐ NO	11. IF NO, ALIEN REGISTRATION NO.	12. FIRST NAME OF EITHER PARENT

13. ELEMENTARY OR HIGH SCHOOL ATTENDED	14. LIST ANY OTHER NAMES EVER USED (Alias Maiden, etc.)	15. PLACE OF EMPLOYMENT (Business Name and Address)	16. WOULD YOU LIKE TO BE AN ORGAN DONOR? ☐ YES ☐ NO

	YES (✓)	NO (✓)	DATE FAILED	REASON FAILED
17. Have you previously failed a driver's license examination in Connecticut?				
18. Have you ever been licensed in another state?		NO. YEARS		LICENSING STATE
19. Is your right to operate a motor vehicle suspended here or in any other state?		SUSPENSION OCCURED IN WHAT STATE?		REASON FOR SUSPENSION
20. Do you now, or have you ever previously held a Connecticut license?		IF YES, IN WHAT YEAR(S)		CONNECTICUT LICENSE NO. (9 digits)
21. Do you wear glasses or contact lenses?				
22. Have you been treated for seizures during the past three years?				
23. Do you have any physical handicaps or disabilities such as emotional problems, chronic illness, addiction to alcohol and/or other drugs that will interfere with your ability to drive?		IF YES, EXPLAIN		

IMPORTANT INSTRUCTIONS: After you have answered the above questions, have the following items ready to show to the Cashier.
(a) **IDENTIFICATION** (proof of name and date of birth).
(b) **DRIVER'S EXAM APPOINTMENT CARD.**
(c) If under 18, parental consent form and proof of completion of an approved Driver Education Course.
(d) **$15.00** fee (cash, check or money order made payable to '**DMV**').

DO NOT WRITE BELOW THIS LINE — OFFICE USE ONLY

PROOF OF IDENTIFICATION	TYPE OF ACCEPTABLE I.D. SHOWN	PREVIOUS LIC. INFORMATION	DRIVER LICENSE NO.	ISSUED BY (State)	EXPIR. DATE

CERTIFICATE OF PARENTAL CONSENT	IF APPLICANT IS A MINOR (age 16-17), PARENT OR GUARDIAN MUST COMPLETE AND SIGN CONSENT CERTIFICATE BELOW.

I hereby request that an operator's license be issued to the minor filing this application.

RELATIONSHIP TO MINOR	SIGNED (Authorized consenter) X

TRAINING — INSTRUCTION

CLASSROOM	SCHOOL NAME		COMM. SCHOOL LIC. NO.	DRIVER ED. CERT NO.
BEHIND THE WHEEL	SCHOOL NAME (If same as above, print "Same")	TRAINING CODE (Circle one) 4 Secondary & Commercial 5 Secondary & Parent Training 7 Parent Training 8 Secondary 9 Commercial		

CERTIFICATION BY APPLICANT (To be signed in presence of Inspector)	I hereby certify that the statements made in this application are true to the best of my knowledge and belief.	WRITTEN SIGNATURE OF APPLICANT X
	STATE OF CONNECTICUT DATE Subscribed before me	SIGNED (Inspector) X

MOTORCYCLE PERMIT	☐ ISSUE PERMIT	DATE	SIGNED (Inspector) X

TEST VEHICLE	MAKE	TYPE (If applicable)	REG. NO. & STATE	REQUIRED PROOF OF INSURANCE SHOWN? ☐ YES ☐ NO	MOTORCYCLE ☐ Applicant wearing safety glasses	☐ MC equipped w/approved windshield

LAW TEST	☐ MACHINE	☐ WRITTEN	☐ ORAL	☐ FOREIGN	TEST NO:	TEST RESULT: ☐ WAIVED ☐ PASSED ☐ FAILED

VISION		BOTH	LEFT	RIGHT	DEPTH/COLOR PERCEPTION
	WITHOUT GLASSES	20	20	20	COLOR PERCEPTION ☐ NORMAL ☐ BELOW NORMAL
	WITH GLASSES	20	20	20	DEPTH PERCEPTION ☐ NORMAL ☐ BELOW NORMAL
	CONTACT LENSES	20	20	20	☐ PASSED ☐ FAILED

LIC. TYPE	OPTICAL	REG.	LIMITED	NO FEE ☐ U.S. SERV. ☐ GOV'T ☐ GOV'T M.C.	SP. EQUIP.	CLASS (Circle) 1 2 3	AND M.C.	M.C. ONLY	DRV. TRG.

ROAD TEST AND LICENSE INFORMATION	☐ WAIVED ☐ PASSED ☐ FAILED	REASON FOR FAILURE: ☐ CONTROL ☐ STEERING ☐ JUDGMENT ☐ TURNS	☐ BACKING ☐ PARKING
	REMARKS	SIGNED (Inspector) X DATE	

Ed Pepper got a new job as a cook. He had to fill out a W-4 form for his new company. He read the instructions and filled out the W-4 form.

Look at Ed's form. Ed filled out the top. That was easy.

Form **W-4** (Rev. January 1985)	Department of the Treasury—Internal Revenue Service **Employee's Withholding Allowance Certificate**	OMB No 1545-0010 Expires: 11-30-87

1 Type or print your full name
Edward Pepper

Home address (number and street or rural route)
222 File Street

City or town, State, and ZIP code
Power City, MA 01202

2 Your social security number
23021 8041

3 Marital Status
☒ Single ☐ Married
☐ Married, but withhold at higher Single rate
Note: If married, but legally separated, or spouse is a nonresident alien, check the Single box.

4 Total number of allowances you are claiming (from line F of the worksheet on page 2) **2**

5 Additional amount, if any, you want deducted from each pay . . . . $ —

6 I claim exemption from withholding because (see instructions and check boxes below that apply):
a ☐ Last year I did not owe any Federal income tax and had a right to a full refund of **ALL** income tax withheld, **AND**
b ☐ This year I do not expect to owe any Federal income tax and expect to have a right to a full refund of **ALL** income tax withheld. If both a and b apply, enter the year effective and "EXEMPT" here ▶ Year
c If you entered "EXEMPT" on line 6b, are you a full-time student? . . . . ☐ Yes ☐ No

Under penalties of perjury, I certify that I am entitled to the number of withholding allowances claimed on this certificate, or if claiming exemption from withholding, that I am entitled to claim the exempt status.
Employee's signature ▶ *Edward Pepper*   Date ▶ *Oct. 15* , 19 *88*

7 Employer's name and address (**Employer: Complete 7, 8, and 9 only if sending to IRS**) | **8** Office code | **9** Employer identification number

Ed's W-4 form

He read question 4. He was not sure of what to write for this question. He asked someone at the company for help. Then he understood it better.

Ed took two **allowances**.
1. A personal allowance for himself
2. A special allowance because he is single and has one job

He drew a line in the box after question 5 because he does not want any other money **deducted** from his pay.

Ed did not answer question 6. He must pay tax. He is not asking to be **exempt**.

He filled in the rest of the form and signed his name. He did not answer questions 7, 8, and 9. These are for his employer to answer.

Practice

Here is a W-4 Form. Fill it out. Ask for help if you need it.

Form **W-4** (Rev. January 1982)	Department of the Treasury—Internal Revenue Service **Employee's Withholding Allowance Certificate**	OMB No. 1545–0010 Expires 4–30–83

1 Type or print your full name	2 Your social security number	

Home address (number and street or rural route) City or town, State, and ZIP code	**3 Marital Status**	☐ Single ☐ Married ☐ Married, but withhold at higher Single rate **Note:** If married, but legally separated, or spouse is a nonresident alien, check the Single box.

4 Total number of allowances you are claiming (from line F of the worksheet on page 2) . . . .

5 Additional amount, if any, you want deducted from each pay . . . . $

6 I claim exemption from withholding because (see instructions and check boxes below that apply):

  a ☐ Last year I did not owe any Federal income tax and had a right to a full refund of **ALL** income tax withheld, **AND**

  b ☐ This year I do not expect to owe any Federal income tax and expect to have a right to a full refund of **ALL** income tax withheld. If both a and b apply, enter "EXEMPT" here . . . . ▶

  c If you entered "EXEMPT" on line 6b, are you a full-time student? . . . . ☐ Yes ☐ No

Under the penalties of perjury, I certify that I am entitled to the number of withholding allowances claimed on this certificate, or if claiming exemption from withholding, that I am entitled to claim the exempt status.

Employee's signature ▶   Date ▶   , 19

7 Employer's name and address (including ZIP code) (FOR EMPLOYER'S USE ONLY)	8 Office code	9 Employer identification number

Check Yourself

Look at your W-4 form again. Did you write it right? Let's see.

Answer these questions. Mark Yes or No.   YES ✔ NO

1. Did you print your name, address, and Social Security number in questions 1 and 2?   ☐ ☐

2. Did you answer questions 3, 4, 5, and 6?   ☐ ☐

3. Did you sign your name next to the arrow?   ☐ ☐

4. Did you answer questions 7 and 8?   ☐ ☐

5. Did you write today's date?   ☐ ☐

10   Health Insurance Application Form

Important Words
Enrollment—joining.
Employee number—identification number given to workers in some companies.
Date of hire—the date that you got your job.
Date of rehire—the date that you got your job again.
Eligible—fits in with the rules.
Attained—reached.
Reverse side—the back.
Coverage—what the insurance plan will pay for.

You know that some doctor's bills and hospital bills are very high. You or someone else in your family may get very sick. Those bills may cost more money than you have.

Most companies have a group health insurance plan. It helps all their employees pay for doctors, hospitals, and medicines. There are many different kinds of plans. Some plans pay for all medical bills. These plans even pay for dentists' bills. Other plans pay for part of the cost. Someone in your company will tell you what kind of insurance plan the company has.

It costs money to have insurance. Sometimes, the employer pays all the insurance costs to the insurance company. In some companies, the employer pays part of the cost. The rest is taken out of the workers' paychecks.

You can also buy your own health insurance. There are many different kinds of plans. Some of them may cost a lot of money. Find out about the different plans and pick the best one for you.

Health Maintenance Organizations

Another kind of health plan is called the Health Maintenance Organization (HMO). You must pay a yearly fee to become a member of an HMO. HMO's have their own doctors. Sometimes they have their own clinics, too. An HMO can take care of all your health needs. When you join an HMO, you must use their doctors and clinics. Your visits to these doctors don't cost very much money.

Sometimes your employer pays the yearly fee. Other times, you have to pay part of the yearly fee and your employer pays the rest. You can also get this kind of health insurance by yourself. Then you have to pay all the fee.

Some companies use HMO insurance for their employees. Other companies use group health insurance. Some big companies have more than one kind of health plan. In these companies you can choose the plan that you want.

Ann Alter had health insurance from her company. But this health plan did not pay for some kinds of doctor bills. Ann's mother also needed health insurance. Ann looked in the Yellow Pages of her telephone book under Health Maintenance Organizations. She called some of the companies in the phone book. Each company told her about its plan. Ann and her mother talked about the different HMO plans. Then they picked one company.

Ann and her mother must each fill out a form. Look at Ann's form. At the top, she filled in her Social Security number. Then she printed her name on the next line. She checked Female and wrote her date of birth.

She checked Southborough because that health center is closest to her home. Ann will use the clinic in that town.

Ann is asking for this insurance for herself, so she checked Individual.

Ann did not write in the gray spaces. The insurance company will fill out these parts.

She went on to the next part. Ann has never been a member of this plan. Her family has never had insurance with this company. Ann checked No for that question. She wrote in her address and telephone number. She drew a line in the space for Billing Address because her home address and her mailing address are the same.

The rest of the form is about dependents. Ann does not have any dependents so she did not fill this in. She wrote the date on the bottom and signed her name.

Non-Group Application

INSTRUCTIONS: Please use pen or typewriter.
Shaded areas are for CHP use only.

Community Health Plan

| 01 | 30 | 0____41111 | Social Security # | 315 06 2908 | 1/2 | 1 | 0 |

| Your Name | Alter LAST | Ann FIRST | Marie MIDDLE | Male ☐ Female ☒ | Date of Birth | MO 3 / DAY 17 / YR 70 |

Please mark your health center choice.*
01 ☐ Kenmore 04 ☐ Wellesley 06 ☐ Braintree 08 ☐ Boston
02 ☐ Cambridge 05 ☐ Medford 07 ☐ Peabody 09 ☒ Southborough
10 ☐ W. Roxbury

Individual ☒   Family ☐

| Effective Date of Coverage | MO. / | DAY / | YR. 02 |

Medical Record #

| Have you or any family member ever been a member of CHP? | ☐ Yes ☒ No | If you or any family member were previously a member under another name, please indicate former name: | |

| 01 | 31 | dup | Home Address: | NUMBER AND STREET 17 Bay Drive |

CITY & STATE Power City MA   ZIP CODE 01202   TELEPHONE (413) 247-6167 HOME _____ WORK

| 01 | 37 | dup | 223 | Billing Address (IF DIFFERENT) | NUMBER & STREET _____ | CITY & STATE | ZIP CODE |

* If dependents choose a different health center, write that center's code number here.
01 ☐ Kenmore 04 ☐ Wellesley 06 ☐ Braintree 08 ☐ Boston 10 ☐ W. Roxbury
02 ☐ Cambridge 05 ☐ Medford 07 ☐ Peabody 09 ☐ Southborough

						Last Name	First	Middle	Sex	Date of Birth	MO. DAY YR. / /	Eff. Date	Medical Record #
01	50	SS#	2	1 2	☐ Husband ☐ Wife	Last Name	First	Middle	Sex	Date of Birth	MO. DAY YR. / /	Eff. Date	Medical Record #
01	50	dup	4	1 2	☐ Son ☐ Daughter	Last Name	First	Middle	Sex	Date of Birth	MO. DAY YR. / /	dup	Medical Record #
01	50	dup	4	1 2	☐ Son ☐ Daughter	Last Name	First	Middle	Sex	Date of Birth	MO. DAY YR. / /	dup	Medical Record #
01	50	dup	4	1 2	☐ Son ☐ Daughter	Last Name	First	Middle	Sex	Date of Birth	MO. DAY YR. / /	dup	Medical Record #
01	50	dup	4	1 2	☐ Son ☐ Daughter	Last Name	First	Middle	Sex	Date of Birth	MO. DAY YR. / /	dup	Medical Record #
01	50	dup	4	1 2	☐ Son ☐ Daughter	Last Name	First	Middle	Sex	Date of Birth	MO. DAY YR. / /	dup	Medical Record #

I understand that, in order to be covered, services must be obtained at the CHP Health Center or in a hospital when a member is admitted or referred by an CHP physician. I understand that benefits for which I (we) will be eligible if accepted for CHP membership are in accordance with those described in the Community Health Plan materials.

Nov. 1, 1988
DATE

Ann Marie Alter
SIGNATURE

M46 A02
8503 15M

Ann's health plan application form

Here is a health plan application form for you to fill in. You are asking for this insurance for the first time. Fill in all the parts for **enrollment**.

Remember that all forms are not the same. Your company may give you a different form.

Blue Cross and Blue Shield of New Jersey

APPLICATION FOR ENROLLMENT OR CHANGE

P.O. Box 420
NEWARK, N.J. 07101

1. APPLICANT'S LAST NAME	FIRST NAME	MID. INIT.	2. SEX (☑) [ ] MALE [ ] FEMALE	FOR PLAN USE ONLY — IDENTIFICATION NO.

3. STREET ADDRESS	CITY	STATE	ZIP CODE	TRANCODE	GROUP NO.

4. GROUP NO.	5. APPLICANT'S BIRTHDATE — MO. DAY YR.	6. EMPLOYEE NO. (IF ANY)	7. SOCIAL SECURITY NO.	EFF. DATE

8A. Date of Full-Time Hire — MO. DAY YR.	8B. Date of Part-Time Hire — MO. DAY YR.	9. DATE OF REHIRE — MO. DAY YR.	10. MARITAL STATUS (☑) [ ] SINGLE [ ] DIVORCED/SEPARATED [ ] MARRIED [ ] WIDOW(ER)	SEX	CON. COV. DATE	DOB

11. GROUP NAME & LOCATION (CITY & STATE)	HSP COV.	MSP COV.	MM COV.	WRAP MM
	COMP HP	RX	DENTAL	VISION	LEGAL

12. Print first name of each dependent. Family dependents eligible and to be included in this application are spouse under age 65 and all unmarried children by birth or legal adoption and stepchildren of applicant who have not attained age 19. Inclusion of a spouse, age 65 or over, is optional.

Names of Eligible Dependents (Do Not Repeat Your Name Below)	Birthdate Mo.	Day	Yr.	Relationship Wife	Hus.	Son	Dau.

13. Type of Contract ↓	BLUE CROSS	BLUE SHIELD	MAJOR MEDICAL	WRAP MM	COMP HP	PRE-SCRIP-TION	DENTAL	VISION	LEGAL
SINGLE									
PARENT & CHILD(REN)									
FAMILY									
HUSBAND & WIFE									

14. Indicate whether you and/or your spouse, if any, are now or will shortly be enrolled under Part A and/or Part B of Medicare.

Check ☑	PART A	PART B
APPLICANT	[ ] Yes [ ] No	[ ] Yes [ ] No
SPOUSE	[ ] Yes [ ] No	[ ] Yes [ ] No

15. Check this box if you have elected your coverage to be primary over Medicare because you are actively employed, your employer has 20 or more employees, and you and or your spouse are between 65 and 69 years of age, as required by TEFRA [ ]

16. If you are reenrolling following completion of military service, complete this section.

DATE ENTERED MILITARY MO. DAY YR.	DISCHARGE DATE MO. DAY YR.	DATE OF MARRIAGE (IF ANY) WHILE IN MILITARY MO. DAY YR.

17. If you are transferring from a Plan outside of New Jersey, enter name of Plan and attach Form 3003. → NAME OF PLAN

APPLICATION FOR ENROLLMENT OR CHANGE

18. If you and/or your spouse, if any, are now enrolled with Blue Cross and/or Blue Shield of N.J., copy the following from your I.D. card:

BLUE CROSS [ ] → / BLUE SHIELD [ ] →	IDENTIFICATION NUMBER	EFFECTIVE DATE	COVERAGE CODE	TYPE	GROUP NO. (IF ANY)	CHECK HERE IF THIS IS NON-GROUP COVERAGE [ ]

19. If you are applying for a change in your contract(s) or wish to enroll your spouse and/or child(ren), complete below: (also complete item 18)

Check below:
[ ] ENROLL SPOUSE
[ ] ENROLL CHILD(REN)
[ ] OTHER (explain) _____

Date of Marriage
Mo. Day Yr.
Maiden Name of Wife

If you are enrolled under Medicare Complementary Coverage, check appropriate box(es)
[ ] SUBSCRIBER OVER 65   [ ] SPOUSE OVER 65
[ ] DISABLED AND UNDER 65
[ ] SUBSCRIBER ACTIVELY EMPLOYED AND ELECTS COVERAGE PRIMARY OVER MEDICARE.

20. If you are terminating enrollment of spouse and/or child(ren), complete below: (also complete item 18)

Person(s) Being Terminated:
[ ] SPOUSE
[ ] CHILD(REN)

Reason(s) for Termination:
[ ] DIVORCE [ ] DEATH [ ] SEPARATION [ ] MEDICARE
[ ] ENTERED MILITARY [ ] CHILD REACHED ELIGIBILITY AGE LIMIT

[ ] OTHER (explain) _____

Date Occurred:
MO. DAY YR.

775 (5-85)

SEE REVERSE SIDE FOR ADDITIONAL IMPORTANT INFORMATION

21. APPLICANT'S LAST NAME FIRST NAME MID. INIT.	22. SEX (☑) [ ] (2) MALE [ ] (9) FEMALE	DO NOT WRITE IN THIS BOX

23. APPLICANT'S BIRTHDATE MO. DAY YR.	24. FIRST NAME OF APPLICANT'S SPOUSE (IF ANY)	

25. GROUP NO.	26. GROUP NAME

27. NAME AND LOCATION (CITY & STATE) OF SPOUSE'S EMPLOYER (IF UNMARRIED OR SPOUSE IS UNEMPLOYED, CHECK "NONE")
[ ] NONE

IF YOU OR YOUR IMMEDIATE FAMILY ARE COVERED BY ANY OTHER GROUP HEALTH INSURANCE PROGRAMS, COMPLETE THE SECTION BELOW. IF NONE, CHECK "NONE". INCLUDE ANY OTHER GROUP HEALTH COVERAGE PROVIDED THROUGH OTHER INSURANCE COMPANIES OR OTHER BLUE CROSS AND/OR BLUE SHIELD GROUP COVERAGE. DO NOT INCLUDE ANY COVERAGE PROVIDED THROUGH THE GROUP NAMED IN ITEM 26.

28. NAME OF OTHER INSURANCE COMPANY
☐ NONE (0)

29. ADDRESS OF OTHER INSURANCE COMPANY – CITY AND STATE

30. NAME OF POLICY HOLDER – LAST AND FIRST	31. POLICY NUMBER OR IDENTIFICATION NUMBER

32. POLICY HOLDER NAMED IN
ITEM 30 IS APPLICANTS: ☐ (9) SELF   ☐ (2) WIFE   ☐ (9) HUSBAND   ☐ (6) DAUGHTER   ☐ (5) SON

DO NOT DETACH ▼   PLEASE BE SURE TO COMPLETE ITEM 33 BELOW   DO NOT DETACH ▼

- -

33. I HEREBY APPLY TO BLUE CROSS AND/OR BLUE SHIELD OF NEW JERSEY FOR COVERAGE ON BEHALF OF MYSELF AND ANY ELIGIBLE DEPENDENTS LISTED ON THE REVERSE SIDE.

I UNDERSTAND AND AGREE THAT ANY COVERAGE PROVIDED PURSUANT TO THIS APPLICATION WILL BE AT THE LEVEL OF BENEFITS AVAILABLE THROUGH ARRANGEMENTS BETWEEN BLUE CROSS AND/OR BLUE SHIELD OF NEW JERSEY AND MY GROUP.

I HEREBY ACCEPT RESPONSIBILITY FOR PAYMENT OF ANY PORTION OF THE PREMIUM, IF APPLICABLE, WHICH I HAVE AGREED TO PAY THROUGH THE GROUP. I FURTHER ACKNOWLEDGE THAT COVERAGE SHALL BECOME EFFECTIVE ONLY IF APPROVED BY BLUE CROSS AND/OR BLUE SHIELD OF NEW JERSEY AND ONLY FOR SUCH HOSPITAL ADMISSIONS WHICH OCCUR, AND SUCH SERVICES WHICH ARE RENDERED ON OR AFTER THE EFFECTIVE DATE OF COVERAGE.

I CERTIFY THAT THE STATEMENTS IN THIS APPLICATION ARE TRUE.

Signature of Applicant _____ Date _____

UPON COMPLETION, RETURN THIS APPLICATION TO YOUR REMITTING AGENT

Check Yourself

Look at your health plan application form. Did you fill it in the right way? Let's see.

Answer these questions. Mark Yes or No.   YES ✔ NO

1. Did you fill in parts 1 to 15?   ☐   ☐

2. Did you draw a line in any parts that have nothing to do with you?   ☐   ☐

3. Did you fill in parts 21 to 28?   ☐   ☐

4. Did you sign the form?   ☐   ☐

Glossary

A

Account title—your name; in a joint account it is all the names on the account.

Acc't—a short way to write account.

Allowance—part of your pay that is not taxed.

Amend—to change.

Applicant—the person that fills out a form.

Application—a form to fill out when you want something.

Attained—reached.

Available—ready to start.

B

Balance—how much money you have left in your bank account.

Bank statement—what the bank sends you every month. It tells all about your checking account for the last month.

C

Cash—money in bills and coins.

Certificate—paper that proves that you did something.

Claim—to say that something is true.

Consent—to say yes.

Coverage—what the insurance plan will pay for.

D

Date of hire—the date that you got your job.

Date of rehire—the date that you got your job again.

Deducted—taken away.

Dependents—you and the people that you take care of.

Deposit—to put money into a bank; the money that you put into a bank.

Duplicate—a copy.

E

Eligible—fits in with the rules.

Employer—the person or company that you will be working for.

Employee—worker.

Employee number—identification number given to workers in some companies.

Endorse—to sign your name.

Enroll—to join.

Enrollment—joining.

Examiner—someone who tests you.

Exactly—just like something else.

Exempt or exempt status—don't have to pay any tax.

Expiration date—the last day that something is good.

F

Felony—a crime.

Female—girl or woman.

Foreign country—not the United States.

Former—past.

Former name—your name as you used to write it.

G

Guardian—someone who takes care of you; not a parent.

H

Hearing impairment—something wrong with your hearing.

Height—how tall you are.

I

Identification—something that proves who you are.

Income tax—a tax on the money that you make from your job.

Initial—the first letter of each part of a name. Formal Ike's initials are F. I.

Instructions—words that tell you how to do something; directions.

Issue—to give out.

J

Joint account—one account for two or more persons.

L

Legal alien—a person from another country. He or she is not an American citizen but is allowed to live here.

Legally eligible—allowed by law.

M

Male—man or boy.

Maiden name—a woman's last name before she was married.

Marital status—married, single, widowed or divorced.

Most recent—the last or newest.

naturalization papers—papers that show that you have become a citizen.

non-resident alien—a person who is not an American citizen and does not live in the United States.

occupation—the kind of work that you do.

operate—to drive.

optional—something that you can do or not do.

original license—the first one.

permanent—for a long time; forever.

personal data—information about yourself. This information can be your age, your address, or other things that tell about you.

physical disability or handicap—something wrong with your body.

position—job.

present age—how old you are now.

presently—now.

previously—before this time.

procure—to get.

provide—to give or supply.

qualifications—things that you do well.

race/ethnic description—the group of people that someone belongs to. A person's race may be black, white, Asian, or other.

rate of pay—how much money someone makes.

receipt—a paper that proves that you gave something to someone.

reciprocity license—a license given in one state because you already have a license from another state.

references—people who know you and can tell about you.

referred by—who told you about this job or how did you find out about it.

refund—you get your money back.

register—to sign up.

relationship—how someone is connected to someone else. It can be a friend, a sister, a brother, an uncle, or another kind of connection.

renewal—bringing a license up to date.

request—to ask for.

requirement—something that you need before you can do something.

Residence—where you live.

Residential address—where you live.

Restored—given back.

Restriction—limit on something.

Reverse side—the back.

Rural route—where a letter carrier delivers the mail outside a city or town.

S

Salary—the amount of money paid for a job.

Satisfaction guaranteed—you can get your money back if you are not happy with what you bought.

Service charges—money that you pay the bank to keep a checking account.

Shipping and handling—the cost of sending things in the mail; this is sometimes called postage and handling.

Signature—your name the way that you always write it. Most people use handwriting—like _Formal Jke_ .

Specify—to tell exactly.

Spouse—your wife or husband.

Suspended or revoked—taken away.

T

Teller—the clerk at the bank window. This person handles your money.

Total—to add up; the whole amount.

V

Voluntary—something that you choose to do or not to do.

W

Withhold—to keep back to pay taxes.

Weight—how many pounds you weigh.

Witness—someone who sees something and tells about it. A witness can be a person who watches someone sign a form.

Abbreviations

Abbreviations for states and territories of the United States:

Alabama	AL	Kentucky	KY	Ohio	OH
Alaska	AK	Louisiana	LA	Oklahoma	OK
Arizona	AZ	Maine	ME	Oregon	OR
Arkansas	AR	Maryland	MD	Pennsylvania	PA
California	CA	Massachusetts	MA	Puerto Rico	PR
Canal Zone	CZ	Michigan	MI	Rhode Island	RI
Colorado	CO	Minnesota	MN	South Carolina	SC
Connecticut	CT	Mississippi	MS	Tennessee	TN
Delaware	DE	Missouri	MO	Texas	TX
District of Columbia	DC	Montana	MT	Utah	UT
Florida	FL	Nebraska	NE	Vermont	VT
Guam	GU	Nevada	NV	Virginia	VA
Hawaii	HI	New Hampshire	NH	Virgin Islands	VI
Idaho	ID	New Jersey	NJ	Washington	WA
Illinois	IL	New Mexico	NM	West Virginia	WV
Indiana	IN	New York	NY	Wisconsin	WI
Iowa	IA	North Carolina	NC	Wyoming	WY
Kansas	KS	North Dakota	ND		

Abbreviations used in addresses:

Apartment	Apt.	Lane	Ln.	Rural Route	RR
Avenue	Ave.	Mountain	Mtn.	South	S.
Boulevard	Blvd.	North	N.	Street	St.
Circle	Cir.	Place	Pl.	Square	Sq.
Court	Ct.	Post Office	PO	Terrace	Terr.
Department	Dept.	Road	Rd.	Turnpike	Tpke.
Drive	Dr.	Route	Rte.	West	W.
East	E.	Rural Delivery	RD		
Highway	Hwy.	Rural Free Delivery	RFD		

Abbreviations used for months and days:

January	Jan.	August	Aug.	Monday	Mon.
February	Feb.	September	Sept.	Tuesday	Tues.
March	Mar.	October	Oct.	Wednesday	Wed.
April	Apr.	November	Nov.	Thursday	Thurs.
May	May	December	Dec.	Friday	Fri.
June	June			Saturday	Sat.
July	July			Sunday	Sun.

Abbreviations used on forms:

Acc't. or Acct.	account	Lic.	license
Amt.	amount	M	male
Apt. no.	apartment number	Mo.	month
Bd.	board	No. or #	number
D.O.B.	date of birth	Rm.	room
F	female	Soc. Sec. No. or SS #	Social Security Number
Ft.	feet	Tel. no.	telephone number
Ht.	height	Yr.	year
In.	inch	Wt.	weight
I.R.S.	Internal Revenue Service	Zip	zip code
Lbs.	pounds		